C000084420

# OPERATION WEREWOL

## **THE COMPLETE TRANSMISSIONS**

### BY
# PAUL WAGGENER

OPWW92/201666FTW

# OPERATION WEREWOLF
## The Complete Transmissions

PAUL WAGGENER

OPWW#001

Copyright © 2016 Paul Waggener

Published by Operation Werewolf

Printed by CreateSpace, An Amazon.com Company

*All Rights Registered by Might.*

First Paperback Edition.

ISBN: 978-0692665954

Cover concept by Paul Waggener & Francisco
Albanese. Layout by Francisco Albanese.

**www.operationwerewolf.com**

Servants of the first Wolf, walking among men
Our cult is fire and frenzy – our Lord is Death.
We are Fear, Might, Ecstasy and Rage;
Crowned Kings of Violence and Power,
Breathlessly charging toward the final Hour.

# Contents

# PREFACE BY JACK DONOVAN

Paul Waggener is a force of nature.

His presence in person and on the written page crackles with energy, vision and authority. With relaxed intensity, he could convince a wandering horde to build an empire or burn one to the ground. A true outlaw spirit, Waggener lives and thinks outside the boundaries of the Empire of Nothing, riding free and shooting straight.

Before I met Waggener or heard him give an interview, I read his work online. His talent as a writer is to infuse the no-bullshit analysis of a tinkering mechanic — does it work, or doesn't it? — with a masculine passion that appeals to every man who was ever a boy who wanted to be bigger than life. He uses the vocabulary of Twentieth Century pulp fantasy to paint verbal Frazettas, whether he is commenting on the spiritual desolation of modernity or inspiring men to harden themselves physically or mentally.

Many have feared and will fear his charisma. Those who cling to the emasculated values of the Empire will be offended by his dark aesthetic, but his doomed sensibility recalls the sagas and the dark humor of men who faced death and who, to their very marrow, understood the cruel joke of life. Waggener gets the joke, but he isn't kidding. He's cynical about the world, but he is completely sincere, and that might be the most offensive thing about his work. In a time when people are so afraid of judgement that they hide behind a series of limp-wristed ironic poses, Paul Waggener's virile veracity is bound to be...unsettling. It's going to make people uncomfortable. He's not trying to be… "cute."

Waggener isn't playing at life, he's living it, and he's writing to inspire others to do the same — to go out and become the kind of men they dreamed about being when they were younger, while they are still breathing.

I count Paul Waggener as a brother, and he inspires me as much as I hope his work will inspire you. I'm glad to see his collected writings in print, though I suspect there will be many more transmissions. Because I know he ain't done writing or fighting yet.

START THE WORLD!

Jack Donovan
March 3, 2016
Cascadia

# FOREWORD

What Is Operation: Werewolf?

OPERATION WEREWOLF IS RABID FUCKING RESISTANCE.

To normalcy, to the drab, the banal, to that disgusting proclivity of the herd-minded to just "fit in."

Although it starts in the gym, or the field, or the workout pit, or the abandoned building you've commandeered in order to perform your daily offerings to the gods of Iron and Blood, Operation Werewolf extends itself far beyond the confines of the weight room.

It is TOTAL LIFE REFORM.

Operation Werewolf is the name that I chose to give to this program, to make it concrete, more real — I became an operative of my own commands, carrying out the edict of Strength and Domination with a merciless determination.

We cannot hope to succeed in this life unless our plan for success and strength is overarching, showing itself True and effective in all areas of our life.

My program's watch-words, "IRON and BLOOD," are words meant to inspire the operative, and to act as indicators of the extremely primal and aggressive nature of my training as well as its two primary tenets: WEIGHTS and DETOXIFICATION OF THE BLOOD.

To stay on the narrow road of Power, I know that I cannot allow myself to slip into week-long excesses of distraction and weakness that will grant me only momentary satisfaction — my goal must be higher, my Will stronger.

This Nietzschean principle, too, is one of the pillars of Operation Werewolf — it is not polite. It does not make excuses for what it is. It is not politically correct. It does not believe that all are equal. It refuses to accept that man has any rights other than what he can take and hold for himself.

This world of theirs has become a disgusting morass of socially dictated "equality," this poisonous creed of All Are One — a perfect tool for those in control, who do not believe it themselves for a second! We are not One. We are not equal. We are individuals, who should be seeking every moment to set ourselves ahead of the swine-herd, to create living Runes of ourselves, god-men and women, capable of great thought and idea as well as epic action and deed.

In order to achieve this, we must have TOTAL LIFE REFORM. Our program must call to the strength principle within us and stir it to wild action — this MUST take place on a physical plane first. In the world of today, thinking is easy and often replaces action entirely. Make of your body a weapon, a thunder-chariot for the will and intellect. In the doing of this task, your Will shall continuously be forged and re-forged, the dross and slag driven from it, hardening alongside your muscle, bad habits cast aside, poor excuses left to bleed out in the dust.

You will Become whatever it is you Desire, and this is the Great Work.

IRON and BLOOD!

# I.
# AN OPERATIONS MANUAL
# FOR A NEW WAR

TRANSMISSION DATE: 11-15-2011

*"Every normal man must be tempted at times to spit on his hands, hoist the black flag, and begin to slit throats."* — H. L. Mencken

We are guerilla warriors, taking our fight to the enemy from deep within his own territory. Our goal? To either separate from this terrain of urban wasteland completely, and live out our lives in newly formed communities which will meet all our social and survival needs without controlling, exploiting or dominating us; or, barring that (since the enemy has taken great measure to keep this from occurring) to lash out at this great machine of control, in order to either a) turn it to rubble or b) make such an inspiring display as to remove fear from the fearful and to Awaken the Sleepers in order to create a massive uprising of these neo-tribes so that our way of life demands to grow and thrive through sheer force of numbers.

Specifically, we seek to do this by example, creating a community based around the ancient archetype of the Wolf Cult in which both men and women are each a leader in their own right, taking their destinies firmly in hand and swearing Oaths to live as heroic examples from which great and legendary stories will spring. We choose to become this heroic example so that others might take the ideal we stand for and fashion it's like in their own image, creating new tribes, cults, elite units of freedom fighters and adventurers, so that across the face of this planet, those of us who feel that deep and mighty calling to something other than the life we have been taught to live can find others of like mind and strong spirit, and that together, through saving and reclaiming our own lives, we can save the entire world. This ongoing project will document the many strands of this idea, showing that through art, culture, community, music and adventure, we can become the heroic archetype that is needed in order to bring this new world about in the ashes of the old one.

# II.

# ROARING WHISPERS

TRANSMISSION DATE: 11-17-2011

*Runegaldr and Norse Cosmology (originally presented as a workshop at Winternights 2009.)*

Today we are discussing the runes, but to do so, we must define loosely what we mean when we use this word. Many of you are familiar with a great deal of information regarding runes, their linguistic and esoteric uses and so on, but we will forge ahead making no assumptions about any of our level of understanding, especially my own.

In their many-layered aspects, the runes are at once letters, ideas, principles, universal mysteries, focus points, meditational guides, and awesome tools for affecting change in both our subjective and objective realities, and it is this last use that we will be attempting to explore here. It would take a great deal more time than we have available to us today to cover what the runes are, and how they can be utilized by one who fully dedicates himself to their mysteries, but perhaps we can meagerly cover one small aspect of it today.

In order to continue with this discussion, we must start by refreshing ourselves a bit with the Norse understanding of cosmology and cosmogony. If we are to understand that on one level the runes are representative of the universe itself, and are seed-forms of the great mysteries of our worlds, we must track that thought to its roots. The connection between runes, galdr and creation is an unmistakable one that cannot be overlooked by any seeker — to study and know the runes is not some archaic form of tarot reading, nor limited to the realms of ritual magic and so on- it is instead an attempt to truly understand this universe we live in, and a struggle to find not only our place in it, but everything else's place as well.

Today however, we are focused on a simpler, smaller aspect of that grandiose and epic task, namely rune-galdr.

The word galdr comes from a root word meaning "to sing or to chant," but is in the ON (*Old Norse*) almost always used in context referring to a charm or spell, and became synonymous later on with anything related to the esoteric — the vocal idea of which translates over beautifully to rune-work, as the etymology of this word "rune" can be traced to the PIE (*Proto Indo-European*) word "reu", which means "to whisper" and "to roar" Ultimately, the word is first found in 4th century Gothic as "runa", meaning "mystery" or "secret". This vibratory and vocal idea permeates the fabric of Norse myth, beginning with the creation itself. As sparks from Muspellheim and ice from Niflheim come together in the great charged space of Ginnungagap, a form takes shape, which is called Ymir. The word Ymir comes from an ON root literally meaning "roarer, or roaring one." and from this great, primal representation of matter and force and vitality and wild potential, the realms are shaped by Odin, and his two brothers Vili and Ve, in an act of sacrificial patricide. Just like knowing the root meaning of Ymir, it is helpful to know that the three brothers who utilize this primal force to create, Odin, Vili and Ve, would translate approximately into our language as "Ecstasy, Will and Holiness." These four combined principles form the groundwork for the thought process and reasoning behind the art of galdr.

From this ancient birth of the realm we exist in, we see matter being willfully formed and shaped from a roaring energy, a vibratory and vocal quality that continues to appear later in the mythology.

The main point to note here is that the roaring by itself forms matter, and transforms the environs around it in a seemingly random, haphazard sort of way, but it is only through ecstatic, inspired energy, will, and sacrality, or wholeness, that a conscious forming and directed creative process is able to take place. This idea carries over to runework directly.in that the rune-forms and sounds by themselves are merely representations — references if you will, to act as a jumping off point for us, a seed from which we can learn, transform, grow, and yes, use to alter, shape and influence our realities, both subjective and objective.

The correlation between vocalization and the runes continues when we look later on in the myths to the point where Odin is hanging from Laerads branches, wounded by spear, and offered to himself in a ritualized sacrifice involving sensory deprivation, pain and fatigue — he peers down into the great depths after hanging there for nine nights, and takes up the runes, the mysteries, the understanding of the universe — and the next verse reiterates this with the famous words "oepandi nam", or " screaming i took them". With a great roar, Odin takes up the mysteries of the worlds, and with that great vocalization, his understanding dawns, and he falls back from there.

While we attempt to experience this same level of enlightenment, we use the vocal forms of the runes as another way of focusing our energies on them, experiencing them fully by immersing ourselves in the stave forms, the lore, our personal interpretations and understanding of them, the vibratory qualities of their sound, and the effect that all this has on us, the world around us, and the worlds within us. We use it to bring our will to bear, choosing specific runes to embody certain principles and thought-forms, and bringing those into the objective world by giving them life through sound and sense, — bringing them from the realm of all-potential into the realm of actual being. Each time we perform this act, we are recreating the holy process of the three brothers, using the roaring, Ymir, to shape and alter their surroundings, their perceptions and their understanding of reality in the way they chose.

While our alotted time here does not allow for us to go completely in-depth into the more advanced workings of rune-galdr, seid galdr and runic formula, we can see that the most utilized form of rune-work is a vocal one — although bindrunes and the like can be carved and stained, and carry a great power on their own, it is primarily through the use of galdr that these staves are understood and actualized on a mystical level — the same can be seen when loading mead, or singing pre-written formulae during the course of ritual and so forth.

There are many runic formulae that have been discovered on various stones, bracteates, amulets and the like, and each of them can be studied and utilized in rune-galdr, as well as formulas of one's own design — in order to fully understand and craft one's own runic formula for use in galdr, there are some basic principles to keep in mind: Throughout the runic aetts, we see that in each aett, there are two vowel forms, each of which represents a core element or property, that can be combined with the more wide and expansive consonant seeds to form complex and layered formula, or working words, which act sort of like the mantras seen in present zen and yogic techniques. Through continued practice and application, there are essentially limitless combinations and principles that can be used to empower and deepen our practice. When creating these formulae, we can look to some historical ones for a better understanding of how this can be done most effectively. As an example of how this functions we will look at the: luwatuwa: formula, originally found on the Vadstena bracteate discovered in 1744. The translation of this word is generally taken to be "to the earth, to the sky," but deeper meanings can be plumbed when we look at its qualities in vocal galdr. When sung in a repetitive manner, new words form themselves in and around the root-word, a deliberate tool which can be seen in other runic formulas such as: lathu: as well as other IE sources in general. (For example, scholars of the Bhagavad Gita have stated that the best way to understand the Gita is to simply vocalize the word over and over, until natural rhythm turns the word into "Tagi." which means "one who has renounced everything for God.") Using this technique within the luwatuwa framework, we can hear a vocal shift in between repetitions, :alu:. So, in this case, we can hear another rune-formula, the popularly inscribed "ALU", within this greater principle. Beside this we can see that there is generally a consonant/vowel/consonant/vowel format, or vice versa, rather than stacking multiple consonants or vowels in a row. Due to this, we can break down the meaning of a formula even more. For example, many are familiar with the Gebo Auja bindrune — combining the two runes :G:::A: together for a meaning of "luck or gift from the gods," On helmets and spears have been found the inscription G A G A G A. We can probably surmise that the formula is not intended to be taken as the word Gagaga, but rather as a formulaic representation of the words Gebo Auja, sort of a runic acronym, if you will.

Galdr is truly a powerful tool, and can offer the practitioner not only a deeper understanding of the runes themselves, but their relations with one another, their vibratory force, and their uses and practical application within the greater work of runic study and esoteric runology in particular. Through its use we can weave a mighty song, and finally begin to ask ourselves the important question: "What would we change, and Why?"

# III.
# (RE)CREATING ORGANIC CULTURE THROUGH MYTH AND RITUAL

TRANSMISSION DATE: 11-22-2011

What are the meanings of ritual and myth? How can the wisdom of our ancestors be applied in a world so completely different from the one in which they lived, loved and told stories? What are the positive effects that these things have on a group of people struggling to create their own mythos?

Myth is the telling of ever-true stories which may have no "historical basis." They are stories from which we gather a meaning, not data or fact, but Truth. They are the stories of gods and heroes, who, like us, faced and overcame adversity and struggle through personal strength and working together with the other incredible individuals within their small communities. They are eternal wisdom, laid out by our ancestors for all time, to be told around fires, to be re-forged and re-fashioned into your own time and place, brought forward as living tradition to learn from as you continually destroy and recreate your own reality.

Ritual is the living of these myths, the connection with their Truths and the vital energy that a direct line to their source brings to the community and the individual. We speak with the voices of gods, knowing that we, too, will become only a story on the lips of future children and ancient storytellers, but that through living a life of heroic might and wonderful Truth, we make undying stories out of our lives and communities.

Through finding a connection with Myth and Ritual, we take back the power of attributing our own meanings to the world around us, shrugging off the ones we have been handed and told are true in favor of our own view and conception of Truth. We use the words and understandings of our ancestors in order to help us find our own — using their words and deeds to lead us to ours. We are living examples of humanity's struggle to find Freedom and Meaning in a world where those words have been packaged and sold back to us with the latest fads and consumerist nonsense — we cast aside these machinations and seek our own place within this vast and alienating universe.

We form community through the identifying with and the desire to continue, those mythologies in which we find common ground with others. We tell those stories to each other, and through the telling, we long to live a life that such stories can be told about — living in an unmediated fashion all the harshness and joy and pain and love that this existence has to offer. We perform and create our own rituals and celebrations, constantly served by and serving our own spiritual need — we are slaves to nothing and no one, least of all our own tradition! It lives and grows with us, like Oak and Ivy, entwined and green so long as we continue to Grow.

Therefore, myth and ritual serve the function of creating and sustaining our organic community, and more, they inspire new growth within those communities, their truths continually unfolding and deepening as we apply them to an ever-changing universe. Live the Myth, and let the living of it become the Ritual of constant Growth and Creation.

*"Hail Day, Hail Day's sons*
*Hail night and her kin.*
*With love, look on us.*
*Send to those sitting here victory.*
*Hail to you gods, and you, goddesses*
*Hail Earth who gives to All.*
*Good spells and speech we ask from you,*
*And healing hands in this life."*

— "Sigrdrifumal," author's translation.

# IV.
# SOWING THE SEEDS
# OF COLLAPSE

TRANSMISSION DATE 11-29-2011

These technomancers weave their web with neon tracers, their empty power spiraling lifelessly out over the electrical waves, the ocean of hunger. Their sorceries are diversions, each new development designed to sustain your interest longer, to captivate not your imagination but your time — your life. A clever device for storing useless data, or another minor convenience that further atrophies the already weakened muscles of self-reliance in our time.

Their incantations use words like "terabyte", "LCD", "hi-def", "RPM." They ply their trade like high tech gypsies, distracting you with tricks while they steal your children and rob you blind, the echoes of their siren song still ringing. They whisper in the ears of world rulers and their contraptions start wars, prolong wars, end wars, start new wars. Everyone wants to kill for the Next Big Thing. Thousand dollar communication devices have taken over our lives. Digital imaging machines that take 200 shots per second make a picture not worth a thousand words, but rather make a thousand pictures not even worth one word. Life is no longer experienced head-on with a ferocious love. It is reviewed in digital format —

each experience merely a pose to later place into the great tentacles of the Internet.

We can escape this grey sickness that has grasped a hold of even the strong, but to do so will require sacrifice: that of our civilization. We as a species have grown pampered and weak, each of us living more comfortably than a thousand kings of antiquity-water, light, heat on command. Food, clothing, gadgetry around every corner for easy consumption. Isolated. Tamed. Controlled. Reliant. Pathetic. Ignorant. Lazy. These are a few of the nicer words that come to mind describing the human condition in present day society. Whether this is because corporate globalization and modern merchant control has dictated this to be our fate, or because we as a people started the snowball effect of ill-advised "progress" and this was its natural outcome is an irrelevant question. All that matters is how we choose to combat this unhealthy, dehumanizing and dominating global situation.

There are more arguments on this front, more words and forums and internet chat rooms and explanations and philosophies and suggested solutions etc. etc. etc. than there are stars in the sky. All of them seem dedicated to whatever the latest buzzword in the modern "anarchist" vocabulary might be, talk upon talk and, unsurprisingly, very little action. This is because the voices on all sides are often of an "all or nothing" slant — one must completely remove oneself from modern society and begin life in a mud hut on Day One, or he must embrace totally the technocratic construct of corporate whoredom and revel in all its might, terror and splendor until his last, smog-filled breath.

The reality is, this "rewilding" is necessary, but must occur on a measured scale of involvement. One cannot simply acquire the skills needed for feral living overnight and move into a hide wikiup the next morning, but nor should s/he succumb to being overwhelmed and give up. There is a natural, more organic method than kicking civilization "cold turkey," that being a slow but steady reintegration and re-education process ultimately leading to a full, well-thought change in lifestyle, worldview and practical living.

It cannot be expected that we close a gap of generation upon generation in a single day, but it can be expected that we END THIS CYCLE NOW, while we are the current generation — otherwise we leave the same sad legacy to our children as our parents left for us: slavery to the system we helped sustain. This is an obvious and horrendous curse to place on our descendants, something to be remedied before we create new life if possible, or to fight tooth and claw so that the children we already have are not faced with the same shackles with which we have been chained for our whole lives.

Breathe deep the richness of the black earth. Run your hands over rough bark, smooth stone, soft fur and remember. Listen to the ragged call of the vulture, the bellow of the elk, the bark of the feral dog and add your voice to this wild wonder. The warm sun on your face, the cold wind in your hair, the wet rain on your back, the full moon shining down on this living earth. This is all the inspiration needed to lay down the supercomputer, the switch, the gear, the machine — and stride boldly and fearlessly back into the Womb of All That Lives. The war is on. Sides are already being chosen. Where do you stand, and what are you achieving for your children and theirs?

# V.

# NEO-TRIBES

TRANSMISSION DATE: 12-1-2011

It is no longer enough to sloganeer and say things thoughtlessly like "smash the state" or "tear it down", without an alternative to the urbanized, mechanized, socialized lifestyle you are struggling against.

Remember: We are attempting to live a heroic lifestyle — but there are others out here in the wasteland that need you to be a hero, to show them that their fears and concerns and dissents are well-founded, and that they, too, can make their own way out of the ruins and into a new way of life that they create for themselves in an unmediated fashion — one that allows, encourages, supports and strengthens instead of crushing, controlling, dominating and debilitating.

The alternative we suggest is the tribal model — a small, self-sustaining, holistic community of equals, all struggling to ensure the good of each individual within that community. This differs from the tired (and often unhealthy or simply non-functional) idea of the "commune" in that instead of what usually degenerates into a bad scene which too often becomes a microcosm of governmental control, or the opposite end of the scale in which no one accepts any accountability and uses buzzwords like "anarchy" as an excuse to be lazy and counter-productive, the tribe is run by a council of its entire membership. Each is held accountable to the other, tribal law is only another word for group consensus, and the entire structure looks inward for strength and determines its own social needs and methods.

We eschew the ideas of "communal ownership" and "worker's unions" and replace them with heroic individuality, personal achievement and the idea that each person is, in fact, unique and has a role to play — knowing what that is part of the exploration. This emphasis on individuality leads to fair treatment in the event of any problem, based on knowing and communicating with one another, allowing the group to deal with situations from a personal standpoint that takes into account things like personality, circumstance and so on, instead of relying on the faceless horror of a "legal system."

We feel that through developing and living the ongoing adventure of this tribal model (which remains in a constantly new and growing state as we deal with the challenges and joys of each day and year) that we can encourage others to develop and grow their own communities and tribes, forming a network of people building small groups to meet their own unique and individual needs as human beings, instead of cog-wheels in that great and terrible machine. Imagine, if you will, tribes of savage and wild hunter/gatherers on the edges of the urban jungle, each one expressing itself through diverse marking and art, rubbing shoulders and exchanging goods in a gifting fashion with small farming communities who have claimed parcels of land for themselves out in the fringes of civilization, living and loving in their own way without fear.

Work is reduced to an often pleasurable group effort instead of a soul-crushing daily horror and the imagined need to rely on the supermarket and corporate giant for our every want becomes a fairy tale for our children.

Before you sneer and shrug these ideas away as "impossibilities," just know that out here in the Wasteland, there are heroes making it a reality, one step at a time.

# VI.
# INTERVIEW WITH GANDVALDR BLÁSKIKKJA

TRANSMISSION DATE: 12-06-2011

What follows is a brief interview with Gandvaldr Bláskikkja, head of an American-based order known as the Galdragildi, which specializes, according to its website is "high-minded Germanic/Teutonic magical study that uses runes, seið, and other esoteric practices. Its aims are toward those of Self-Initiation and whole awareness through accurate investigation and information that is put into practice within one's daily life: where the practice and living of the method are as important as the process of growing."

I had the opportunity to conduct this interview with him at the start of the Yule Season, 2011, and found the answers well-spoken and enlightening.

1: *For those entirely ignorant on the subject, please briefly describe the idea of what you mean when you say Germanic magical study.*

[GB] When referring to terms like "Germanic", it must first be known by the layperson this in no way connotes an approach to Nazi political affiliations or hatred-based racism. The use of "Germanic" as a noun relates to Teutonic folk and their descendants. However when addressing a reference to "Germanic magic", this confers an array of potential focal points specific to the Indo-European families: German, Dutch, English, Scandinavia, etc., and the more esoteric or extinct Gothic foundations, and their spiritual/magical convention. These practices include understanding and use of runes specifically, and may encompass galdrastafur (Icelandic magical signs), fjölkyngi (black art, sorcery), hamramr (shape-shifting), hexology (German hex signs), seið (sorcery, charms), spá (prophecy) in addition to the study and use of entheogens and leechcraft.

2: *Why is what you do and teach still relevant in the modern world?*

[GB] I'm very glad you asked this question. I'll try to present my answer in a way that is understood not only by those already knowledgable with the subject matters mentioned above, but one that will also enlighten those who are unfamiliar. The study and, more importantly, the practice of Germanic magical and spiritual knowledge is no less relevant than eastern martial arts or common contemporary spiritual areas. One typically chooses to follow an eastern path of martial arts: karate, aikido, ju-jitsu, kendo, kempo, tae kwon do, tai chi, kung fu … (the list is nearly endless) because they are seeking to not only learn to defend themselves but to also find a peace or balance within themselves: harmonize within and without for an overall stronger sense of self. The same may be said for those fol owing a religion or spiritual path like christianity, judaism, buddhism, taoism, kabbalah, sufism, muslim...The choice to walk into a martial training hall, or temple, or simply to pick up a book and begin reading about any of these things mentioned is, for most, a sensible selection. These things, after all, are deeply established, time-tested and, for practices with objective results like learning a martial art, it provides the student with nearly immediate feedback — proven through growth and improvement. There are clearly defined levels of progress and goals laid out for them to achieve.

Taking a wholly more spiritual path, like a religious practice, is one generally arrived at due to historic, ethnic, or a germinating seed within (or for some it is asserted upon the individual, i.e. forced conversion). Typically one has a feel for their choice, an intrinsic pull, whether 'faith' or intellect draws them, there is a connection or duty.

Choosing to pursue the Germanic magical (or spiritual) path is no different. What has been put forth in the Galdragildi is a manner of teaching and sharing the experiences of others through leveled progression and achievement.

The model used is the ancient gild system: apprentice, journeyman, master. The development of the individual, if the teachings are actually put to practice: known and understood, are verifiably real with measure and merit. I stress this statement "put to practice" because like any other endeavor: music, martial arts, hunting, etc., there wil be no improvement without adherence to the skills required to master these things. One can carry a violin around with them at all times and onlookers will probably perceive them differently; thinking they must know how to play and indeed be particularly dedicated since they carry the instrument with them everywhere they go. This person with the violin might even be very well-versed in its assembly, care, history and design. However, if they do not spend time correctly applying the bow and fingers to the strings, then they are merely a showman (or woman) deluding others, and more sadly, deceiving themselves into thinking they are truly participating in a history of individuals who have excel ed as musicians. It is very easy to look the part of some greater thing, but as the Hávamál presents to us it is better for a fool to remain quiet than to talk (or show) too much and prove himself lacking.

Still, there are those who are comfortable being a part of the gild system and find their own satisfaction amid learned others without continuing to seek progression toward mastery. This is acceptable as long as one understands that self-imposed limitations will preclude them from taking part in everything the gild has to offer. Naturally, more time and energy is spent on continuous progress and those pursuing such aims. This is in no way a manner of punishment or even a kind of subtle denial. It is simply a matter of time and attention to ensure those who are seeking to stretch themselves and attain greater levels of understanding are being provided with the materials and rewards due their level of accomplishment.

How is this relevant — this area of study and practice? With the focus of higher education being more focused with what is 'new' and 'useful', that is, what can make money or what sates the current political catch-phrases of the year, other areas like the study of religions (other than christianity, muslim, judaism, buddhism), especially those pertaining to Germanic areas, are being swept under the table as antiquated subjects. There are innumerable persons of Germanic Indo-European descent who are turning to completely foreign areas of spiritual development and 'mystic' approach due to lack of awareness or availability of something closer to their hearts and minds. Either this, or pressure is being placed to conform to a more "popular" or "accepted" religion rather than the old ways which are disregarded as primitive (in a negative way) and out-dated. I, for one, have never understood why one would want to be viewed as a member of a "flock" of "sheep" while submitting to the will of some desert-deity teaching philosophies of unconditional love with eternal damnation for being born into a world where all beings are filled with "sin."

Our (Germanic) practices and teachings are viewed as being primitive, or ignorant, but I have personally met some of the most brilliant and insightful individuals who live and grow through these "primitive" endeavors. Likewise, I have also met some of the most desperately lost, weak and self-less (not a compliment) minds who are affiliated with more accepted, common paths.

3: *How do these practices truly aid in shaping the individual, and can you discuss how an individual might improve their life with this knowledge/practice?*
[GB] Inferred above through the statement of "putting to practice", the participant of this path work would first need to learn how to inspect themselves

on a very objective level; not merely seeing the areas in their life where they are weak or desire improvement, but also to gauge their strengths which will support and drive them forward. From there, through the activities of the Apprentice, one learns how to apply themselves to measured order and creating a disciplined lifestyle while sharpening their analytical skills: being able to separate the slag from the steel, or wheat from the chaff, so to say, so one can perceive what is truly valuable or useful, and what is merely dross.

Using the investigation of the mysteries (runes) as the foundational points of meditation and energetic expression, the student support consanguinity with the Self (sjalfur sjalfum mér), learning to apply these energies to their lives and hone the way they Need to express. Further along, they may elect to become more 'natural' in their personal approach or decidedly un-natural; but with wholeness of understanding their path. If one takes to heart for proof (that is the archaic definition: a test or trial) of what is being provided, the mindfulness of their work will surely shape their lives — the physical presentation and disciplined accord of mind(s), breath(s) and body in its varied facet and function. Real understanding of the self (and Self) presents the malleable fabrics which can be woven to will. Paths open; roads and rivers now accessible. Now, I'm not being misleadingly cryptic; carrying a violin around while posturing. It would be easy to be delusive and wax with example after example, to talk a good game, but the truth is that it's a hard way and laden with opportunities for self-delusion. People want to feel they are making progress in the best possible means. Being disillusioned hurts, but really there is no greater thing than to have lost one's illusions and to begin to see what is beyond the subjective mirror. This isn't implying persons will be pristine in all aspects of their health and lives, but that awareness and commitment will be at the forefront. A person who smokes may continue to, but rather than blame others (addiction, tobacco cos., poor parental guidance) they will maintain ownership and awareness of their own actions: fully informed and accepting the causes and effects. They may choose to quit, or they may choose to continue smoking; no blame, no uncontrollable force.

4: *What is a Black School/Lodge?*

[GB] A "black school" as referring to the Galdragildi and its activities is reserved for the higher work of the gild. One facet of this is a reflection of the legendary Black School of Iceland where the students were said to be instructed directly by the devil. Students attending such a mythical school put aside all other interests and distractions to focus wholly (holy) upon obtaining esoteric knowledge from otherworldly beings. The reference point to this is one of extreme dedication and sacrifice for one's personal attainment.

Considering the "black school" in relation to "white" vs. "black" magic — the black school is a place of Self-ish exploration and elevation. There is little worse than a person who is self-less: thinking little of their own needs and supposedly caring only for others, having no connection or understanding of their own path, desires, influences. They seek to meddle and manipulate all under the pretense of having others' in their best interest. The "black school/lodge" is a place where one deeply delves into their own investigation (as mentioned above) and asserts their Will for transformation (among other things). There are no preconceptions of "good" or "evil" (which by some schools of thought would cause one to automatically be placed into the "Evil" category), there is will and intention. Óðinn enacts his will to obtain what he Needs. For this, the All-father is considered by many to be evil and in fact takes the name Evil-doer (Bólverkr) for during some of his efforts. Freyja gave herself to dwarves so she may win the desirable Brisingamen necklace. The Eddas, prose and poetic, are replete with examples of these entities performing tasks that, by some narrow standards, would be considered unscrupulous, grim or nefarious.

However they come through their particular tasks having completed something exceeding their own breadth of desire or fulfillment; a measure of greatness and resounding value.

5: *What are your aims for the future of your school?*

[GB] Any plans for permanent structures, area growth, etc. are obvious directions for any organization. I was asked this question by one of the founding members a couple of years ago, and my answer is still the same. As succinctly as I can put it, the gild must grow and survive beyond my own life. It is easy to manage an organization for a brief time and obtain short-term successes, but for the Galdragildi to be ultimately successful, it must exist beyond our lives; passing through the current leader(s) hands into those who are currently following (or have followed) what the gild offers wholly.

It's not about having hundreds of members worldwide. What good would that do, really other than make the gild popular? In fact, I've considered closing membership for a time in order to focus on the current participation, and even then, only taking in a very limited amount of members per year. That way, my ultimate aim of a generational gild presence would be more likely assured. I don't look at this as a re-awakening, or re-establishing of things. It's not about popularity, it's about continuing the traditions and practices of our ancestors with integrity and a deepening sense of awareness of them (our ancestors) and the gods, goddesses, and spirit folk, and more specifically, awareness of the individual.

Thanks for the opportunity to respond to these questions. I hope they are satisfactory and not too far off the heart of what was being asked.

Uppreisn gegn náttúrunni og sjá að ég er vil t eins og heilbrigður. (Rebel against the wild and see that I am wild as well.)

Gandvaldr Bláskikkja

— gildmaster

# VII.

# INTO THE DARK FOREST

TRANSMISSION DATE: 11/20/2012

The civilized world around us is dying. The towering constructs of capitalism, mass urbanization and globalized control are rotting from within and cannot sustain themselves for much longer; and when they fall, the human that has been created by them will find himself in a terrifying, unfamiliar new reality.

This reality will be one of brutal extremes-upheaval always leads to the unavoidable violence and aggression that is human nature, a nature that has remained true even in the face of generations of social conditioning. It will be a time where the currency of the money-driven world will be useless and devoid of meaning- focus will again shift to the three things that humans have always needed: sustenance, clothing, shelter. Because of this, the individual's skill-sets and personal fortitude will decide his real worth — not his car, his bank account, his sense of fashion.

What the civilized man would look on with fear and trepidation, a raw, gnawing terror at the knowledge that in a world like this, he would die of hunger, of exposure, of murder, or countless other dangers, we look upon with an understanding that the world has always been this way and must always return to it. We recognize the fact that the whoremongers of corporate culture are poisoners, reckless ruiners of the natural world, purveyors of weakness, perversion and decadence and are fit only for the grim end of a cold, shallow grave.

Through this realization, that we are being deliberately herded, weakened and poisoned, treated not as human, but as herd animal, we find ourselves wondering: what is the answer to this blatant disrespect and mistreatment?

And we answer, that the only proper response is to not only bite back, but to break the chains and remove ourselves from this great grinding machine of mindless labor, consumption and waste.

The way that we believe this needs to be done is in deliberate community. Tribes that exist to support, to train, to re-connect the individual with his wild nature and to foster and build relationships based not on politically correct rhetoric or artificial social structures but on the true realities that mankind has lived for aeons. The Wolves exist out on The Edge: we prowl the shadows at the end of the world you know, marking a transition point into the Dark Forest of an ancient way made new again, brought forth from the primal places of our species past and made relevant again through Need.

We see this time of Change as not only a welcome thing, but a necessary one. It re-awakens our desires to make ourselves more than we are, god-men emulating the age-old archetype of the Wolf God, supermen attempting to go beyond the current evolution of mankind and become something greater.

But in order to survive this Change, it is mandatory that we begin our evolution toward this way of life NOW. Our bodies must be lean, hard and free of poison. Our minds must be clear and unfogged with the distractions of technological addiction, substance abuse and rulership dependency. Our spirits have a need to be re-connected with the ancient ancestral ritual and primal drive that comes from a rewilding of the soul, a lust for the freedoms and savagery of the natural world and our place in it as symbiote, not parasite.

This will be achieved in our lifetime. We will see our children and our tribesmen's children stalking the deer, knowing the joy of the hunt and the kill, wearing the skins of animals they have slain. We will look with pride and joy on the smoking ruin of the filthy world these enslavers have built, turning our backs on it and striding back into the unmediated existence we have created for ourselves, howling the songs of Growth and Renewal into the clear winter skies. But it will only be achieved through action: a revolution of mind and lifestyle that leads in a clear path AWAY from this system we currently all support. It must be a total life-reform that changes the way we think, act, live and love, and it must begin now.

# VIII.
# THE IRON IS NOT MY FRIEND

TRANSMISSION DATE: 9/26/13

When I lift, the iron is not my friend. It is an obstacle — a hated enemy standing defiantly between me and my goal of self-overcoming. As I focus in on it with grim determination, it transforms; from simple steel, it takes on the face of a man I hate, a former friend who betrayed me, an imagined individual prepared to rape my mother or murder my brother. As it transforms, it transforms me, as well. I take on the aspect of the snarling wolf- feral aggression courses through my expanding veins. I am a berserker! One foot on the prow of a longship, biting the metal edge of my shield in ravenous anticipation of impending carnage. I am the ferocity of Rudra's destroying nature. I am the thunder of charging hooves and the reckless might of the raging storm.

From here, I challenge the laws of the very cosmos. I defy this Earth's gravitational pull, outdoing it with nothing more than the strength of my arm-sinew and muscle straining against reason and probability, discarding ideas of impossibility and likelihood with a savage growl of supreme exertion...barbaric instinct challenging and dominating the intellect.

This is why I lift — not for competition, save with myself and the elemental forces. Not for aesthetic, save that natural beauty that comes from real strength. Not for beast, devil or god, save that god that lies within, that beast that stirs and slavers when he is roused by challenge; that devil that sneers at weakness and whispers promises of the power and dominion that comes with defeating it.

When we call lifting "training", what is it that we are training for?

Certainly, if you compete with other lifters, this word is simply applicable, but otherwise, its use requires validation. That validation is this: to lift is to become Strong. Training for all lifes hardships and battles through a forging not only of body, but of the Will, tearing down those obstacles, however impassable they seem, through a murderous and fanatical devotion to Overcome All. The Iron is not my friend — it is a foe to conquer. Lift, eat, fight, fuck.

IRON AND BLOOD.

# IX.
# ON FIGHTING AND FEROCITY

TRANSMISSION DATE: 10-20-13

Since I was a kid, I have never gone more than a year without being in a fist fight — or more accurately, several.

Some would say that this means I have an antagonistic nature, or that I needlessly place myself in situations that call for violence, or are likely to end in violence — this may be true, but I believe the root is deeper than that. I believe that the so-called "civilized" world is having their violence mediated and spoon-fed to them, just like every other thing these days, and that fewer and fewer people each year have any direct experience with physical hostility.

It's not likely to win me many friends to say this (and who the fuck needs'em?), but I believe that a violent and aggressive nature is essential to being a man, and those who have no first-hand accounts of bone-crunching and concussion-inducing encounters are missing out on one of the crucial aspects of the masculine experience.

This belief is not a priori — it stems from a lifelong unwillingness to take shit, to be treated in an inferior or disrespectful fashion by people who thought that they could say or do whatever they wanted with no repercussion, a trend that continues to worsen as the age-old game of pugilism between men becomes less common anywhere than the ring or on TV.

Some would say that this reduction is due to a fear of increasing legal punitive measures, but I would argue that what can be credited is rather an increasing fear of actually being in a violent situation in general. The more uncomfortable an individual is with the notion of violence, the more terror-stricken he is when put face-to-face with naked aggression.

The term "gameness", used in dog-fighting, refers to a dog's willingness to get in there and fight, and to keep fighting. In other words, it refers to "the size of fight in the dog." This trait is something that we should cultivate in ourselves- no man is born with lesser or greater gameness, it is built from experience, from placing oneself in situations where it must proven, and then making the decision to prove it- hard.

Often, folks seem to think that in the world we live in, there is no need to be this way, that it is a savagery left over from a bygone age, a backward age, which the enlightenment of civilization has freed us from. They view every fight or brawl between men as "ridiculous ego-posturing" or "ignorant chest-pounding." These individuals are likely unfamiliar with Orwell's quote:

> *"Those who 'abjure' violence can only do so because others are committing violence on their behalf."*

This world is a violent place, and just because one person has been fortunate/cowardly enough to avoid any direct contact with that violence, does not mean we have all been so fortunate, or so cowardly. The same people who "abjure violence" on a basic level still watch television shows and idolize those characters who take shit from no one, who solve their problems with violence, who punch out some prick who grabbed their girl's ass at a bar — they idolize them in a quiet, pathetic way, wishing to themselves "if only I could be more like that." Then, the next time someone shoulders them out of the way, disrespects them, manhandles their woman, or whatever, the fear rises up in their belly like a watersnake, and they hide their masculinity away behind a cloak of intellectual scorn, saying "I'm bigger than that. This isn't worth fighting over. Violence is ignorant."

My question, then, is this: what the fuck is worth fighting over? If blatant disrespect to yourself, your significant other, your friends, your family isn't worth it, what is? More importantly, what the hell do you think you'll be able to do about it when you finally decide, "this is worth it." You will attack the situation with the fear that comes from traversing wholly unfamiliar terrain, you will flail wildly, you will be unaccustomed to taking the shock of a punch, or other serious physical trauma. You will likely lose. And if on that day, it truly did matter, you'll have failed yourself and whoever you were fighting for, because you'd lived your life without gameness from day 1.

I'd advise you to start finding out about yourself in a way that only primitive conflict can show you. Get fierce, or get fucked.

*"Barbarians are much more polite than civilized men, since civilized men do not think, as a matter of course, that they may have their skulls cloven in twain."* — Conan

# X.
# LIVING MYTH

TRANSMISSION DATE: 10/27/13

Paganism is wrapped heavily in a shroud of myth, that is, the early stories of a culture relating to social phenomenon and supernatural events, often involving cosmogony and cosmology within the scope of its telling.

The world begins from its simple origins, it becomes, is shaped and peopled by a group of gods — they fight and fuck and love and live and die, and the tales of these things make up that culture's mythology. The stories are told, retold, changed, added to, lost, recreated and told again in the flowing years that make up the great river of a culture's time on this living earth…and yet, somehow, at certain points in those time-rivers, people snatch ahold of a certain telling of these stories, and choose to hold them as dogma, as literal truth, accepting no other way, no other interpretation as holding that Truth with a capital "T".

This idiocy is seen just as often in paganism as it is in those towering monoliths of ignorance and fear that make up monotheism.

Folks clutch at "the lore" or this saga or that saga, and they adhere to the things written therein as though it were objectively "real," using occurrences and happenings in those disty old tomes as justification or explanation or validation for their current practice, now. Here. At least one thousand years later. After the book that they are using for their justification has been filtered through whatever motivations its writer had for putting it down on paper and on and on and on.

The point is, all this weighing of the "truth", all this interpretation, all this study of this word or that word and its accompanying declension or conjugation to sleuth out some obscure passage — what is it accomplishing in YOUR life? What is this obsession with "correctness to the past" worth, at the end of the day? How many fucks can we give about being "authentic to the past," if we are caught up in cracking the longbones of today, our time, and sucking out the marrow? And why would we want to? Why should we do other than pay grim homage to the past, acknowledging our ancestors deeds by raising a horn to them, and then out-doing them, to show that we have not let them down, but taken their blood further afield, stretched the legend of their line long, and lived with blood on our teeth and scalps in our hand.

To be a slave to the past is to forfeit your inheritance, the present. This is OUR TIME. It is given to us to retell the myths with our brief existence here, and to retell them with a fury and lust and a roaring of wild life that cannot be ignored — that will make us legends.

I am not a follower of Odhinn — I am Odhinn. His name means "the ecstasy, the frenzy, the fury, the wild." I am that, and no one can take it from me. I live my life as its own tale, with one foot in each world, drinking, carousing, living and loving, fighting and fucking and raving and rending — my words are spells that reach from the roots into heaven, and the brothers I have chosen are wild Wolves. Sometimes I see them from the edge of our ritual circle in the forest, and I see their shapes change from men to animals, and back to men again, twisting in the firelight like strange beasts, unknown to the weak and civilized man. I look at them, covered in blood and ash, wild eyes, pupils dilated from a mixture of mead and mushroom. I hear their songs ring out through the changing of the year, and I know that THIS is paganism. This is legend. These are the tales that I will remember.

# XI.
# INDIVIDUALITY WITHIN THE COLLECTIVE

## TRANSMISSION DATE: 10-29-13

For a lot of people in this world, the idea of joining a club or organization goes against their personal ideas of individuality and freedom — they'd rather go it alone, not having to worry about rules and regulations, or the responsibility of having to answer to other people in a collective.

Often times, I think what these folks are afraid of the most is assimilation — they feel that if they were to join a club, they would lose all those little things that make them stand out from the crowd in civilian life, and they would just be one of many, rather than the special and unique snowflake they believe themselves to be.

In some cases, this is true — those folks who rely on their little quirks or fashion statements and call that "individuality" are full of shit; they think that a "look" or a gimmick is being an individual, and such is not the case. These types of people are always the first to rail against group or collective, a defense mechanism designed to keep them from having to really test themselves at a higher standard than they are accustomed to.

As always, I refer to the dictionary definition of "individuality" first: "...the quality or character of a particular person or thing that distinguishes them from others of the same kind, esp. when strongly marked."

Here, individuality is referring to strong marks of distinguishing character that make someone stand out from others of the same mold — and therein lies the real challenge of being a member of a club or organization of like-minded people: you have to work your ass off to stand out from the crowd, and this is a desirable thing to everyone involved.

If anything, individuality becomes more marked and obvious within a collective, as everyone strives to find their niche, their area of expertise and really "own" it, which forces them to operate at an extremely high level of dedication and focus, driven by a desire to not fall into a "rank and file" classification. This in turn leads to a more highly functioning individual, someone who, through having to fight for his place within the group, can then easily master the challenges and go far above the bar of general life outside his club.

This assimilation fear is the same terror that strikes the heart of those who never wish their abilities, their mental prowess or physical toughness to be put to the test publicly — they shy away from those people and situations that force them to put their money where their mouth is; most folks would rather let their mouth and their ego run the game, talking endless amounts of shit they know they'll never have to back up. The individual within the collective is much harder than this, as he knows his boasts and claims will constantly be challenged by other strong, uncompromising individuals, who will force him to live up to his words with actions.

This is probably the most important divergence of group vs. "lone wolf" dichotomy — the lone wolf can live his entire life without being challenged or tested. The pack wolf's entire life is one of challenge, ordeal, trial and overcoming. This is not to imply that there are no examples of lone wolves who have lived lives of complete savage strength, shining examples to victory and triumph — it is merely pointing out that to do so alone requires an incredible amount of drive and self-determination that many are not born with, but can learn in a pack setting.

The group setting is neither debasing nor relegates anyone to less than desirous status within itself — any organization needs more than just "a town full of blacksmiths." It takes a lot of different personality types and skill-sets to keep a group running, no matter whether we are referring to a small business or a motorcycle club. Beyond just followers and leaders, there are sub-sets of the human personality type, many of which are extremely useful to bringing forward the entire crew.

What can you offer? What is your area of specialization, and how can it be utilized to benefit the tribe?

The answers to these questions should be sought out and tested, honed to maximum efficiency, and brought to bear as a precision tool to represent your organization with pride, strength and honor.

# XII.
# I HAVE CREATED MY GODS

TRANSMISSION DATE: 12-3-13

I have created my gods. They may share names or basic functions with those deified ideas that have gone before in my ancestral line, names like Odin, Thor, Rudra, Shiva... ecstatically inspired wild men, creators, destroyers, leaders, witch-kings, warriors and killers. But whatever they share, they have been reimagined, reforged in the fires of my own consciousness, to perform the functions that I need them to perform — just as all men have done for thousands of years, but that few men will admit to having done. This practice is central to the difference between a spirituality based around faith or belief, and one based around knowing and certainty. The only "spiritual truths" that exist are the ones we have chosen as true for ourselves — the only certainty in this world are the things we have chosen to be certain of.

Belief is a noun that holds the meaning of "accepting that a statement is true or that something exists." By this definition, belief is essentially synonymous with "hope," which is defined as "the state which promotes the desire of positive outcomes," or "the act of looking forward to something with desire and reasonable confidence. "Desire of positive outcomes. Looking forward to something with reasonable confidence. After looking at these definitions, it would seem that the very idea of hope is not the antithesis to despair, but to Will. Hope is as empty a concept as has ever been conceived, a future-dwelling mindset that looks toward an outcome with a greeting card sentimentality — when applied to religion, it induces the same feelings uncertainty and lack of confidence; a sort of wishing well style spiritual practice: "if I do this or say this, then I HOPE this will happen."

This makes belief, in the religious sense of the word, absurd, naïve, and weak. In what other realm of your life would you apply this terminology where it would not be construed as such? Would you simply accept the idea that 1+1=3? Would you hope with a reasonable confidence that you could bench press 300 pounds? Would you look with a desire for positive outcome at a fistfight between you and a 220 pound juggernaut? No, you would determine the validity and reason of these statements by a series of tests and trials in order to know the truth — in the same way, this process can be applied to our spiritual lives.

Why would I choose to believe a thing, when I could know a thing? What strength could I possibly gain through acceptance that I could not gain tenfold through challenge? What god could I believe in, or choose to believe in, when I have the option to know one?

My gods are created, not in my image, but in the image that I wish to become — this places my foot on the first step of a lifelong journey, not to worship my gods through obeisance and debasement, but through emulation and becoming, worshiping by every deed, praying with every word, offering myself to my Self. To reach the hands outward and upward in a plea for "mercy" or "blessing" bears the stench of rank weakness and the desire to be pulled along like a child reaching upward to a parent to carry them. As strong men, we have nowhere to reach but within. Our gods must live within us, as real as our beating hearts, to provide an emulatable archetype that is as unfailing as the north star.

Do not look on this road and say in pride and hubris, "I am a living god," but rather, with humility and strength and tenacity, say, "I am a wayfarer on a road whose end is certain, but not yet in sight. I will traverse this path with honor, and with courage, and with an indomitable will powered by that Inner Flame which is undying and unquenchable. I am. I will. I will. I am." Keep Rising.

# XIII.
# THE PRIMAL CULT

## TRANSMISSION DATE 12-5-13

There remains a great :N:eed, now more than ever, for a genuine answer to the ragged cry that rises up from deep within the man of Northern ancestry for spiritual fulfillment. In our time, this Wolf Age — what some would call the Kali Yuga, or others, the final stages of a Ragnarok — where there are questions and uncertainties abounding, with few answers and glittering distraction everywhere, we must look deeply into ourselves and the natural world around us to find these answers.

Beginning this task is arduous and difficult, as withdrawal pains from any hard drug can be- moving away from the accepted status quo and striding into a literal and spiritual wilderness, we will experience the pangs of separation, the gnawing desire to return to our comfort zones, the maddening thirst for distraction, shadow, illusion — but if we are to find Truth, we must cling to tenacity and strength as our watchwords. These first steps will be the hardest we have ever taken, but for he who continues and does not falter in his journey of becoming, they will be the most rewarding, also.

For the those of Northern blood, the religions of the East are insufficient to fill that :N:eed, and will forever be a poor and shabby replacement for that which his hot blood calls out for — no matter what he may tell himself, he was meant for something better. Likewise, high-minded and endless intellectual pursuits become a constant phantom, leading always to more questions, an endless pile of books with one foundation constantly seeking to topple the other.

Too often, this leads to a life of highly intelligent inaction, impotence in extremis, the mind sharp and dexterous, the body and will atrophied and feeble.

Even when one looks to the texts and "scriptures" of the Indo-Europeans, the great epics of the Aryan or Icelander, German or Roman — there is a break in the connection of a thousand years that cannot simply be closed overnight — the man of today who reads them is unable to comprehend or apply their wisdom in the same way that he would have then, not to mention the complexity of some of the systems mentioned had become as corrupt as any modern day dogma, existing for control and personal power, not the liberation that we are seeking on this road.

This disconnect must be addressed by "resetting the circuits" as it were, completely burning off what has been accumulated, and starting fresh, head on.

What is being suggested here?

A return to the primitive cult — ritually intoxicated, they cast off the trappings of the civilized world, finding truth in direct experience with their own savage nature. Through identifying with the primal roots of our people —the worship of sun and moon, wolf and bear, they come to an honest faith. A belief in what can be seen and valued for what it is, what it does — an actual and literal belief in man's visible connection with his surroundings, unconcerned and unencumbered with foreign dogma or morality.

Deifying the natural elements, and both the life-giving and the destroying principles existent in the wild- worshiping through an understanding, understanding through a constant and close proximity. Avoiding the entanglements of linguistic shortcoming and the wily poison of metaphor and irony, they speak Truth into existence, creating the world anew in simplicity and terrible beauty.

Gone is the need to debate the value of this metaphysical technique or that, or to explore the latest fad; their communal nature is a tightly knit order of those who Know. With the aid of :ALU: and the many plant allies at the beck and call of the way-wise, they see beyond the borders and hold :AWE: in the palms of their hands — untarnished, unblemished by over-intellectualized banter, their way remains lit by the everburning flames of Joy and Wonder.

The stumbling blocks of cosmogony and cosmology vanish in the simple contemplation of the tree; from a seed :H: we have grown, and spread our branches outward to the heavens, streaming sunward until our time is passed and our spark extinguished, transforming into humus on the forest floor of the ages, feeding new growth, new life, new death.

Our way is simple.
It is direct.
Savage.
Awful.
LIVING.
Hail the Wolves.

# XIV.
# STOP WORRYING AND
# START THE WORLD

TRANSMISSION DATE: 12-29-13

*How I Learned To Stop Worrying
And Start The World*

Far too often in the arena of tribal discussion, or when conversing about how to start the "gang of men" that Jack Donovan champions in his book "The Way of Men," words leads to more words instead of planning and execution. This is a major problem.

It seems like people these days would rather discuss an idea endlessly, weighing its pros, its cons, theorizing about how this or that would happen in hypothetical situations argued about by folks who sometimes may have little to no real world experience in the topics they are arguing about — usually on the internet, where the vast majority of these talks occur — another problem, but one that has been addressed many times.

Pretty soon, these conversations have gone off on a tangent, and spawned new conversations, more arguments, more hypotheticals. Nothing comes of the things discussed in the prior talks, because now the same people are too engaged in winning their war of words in this next one. It brings to mind the guy we've probably all had run-ins with, what I call the "internet lifter." This guy knows everything about the chemical compounds of the latest pre-workout, has an infinite amount of technical knowledge on how you should go about a Romanian deadlift with the proper form, can school you about the myriad ways to get your protein intake up to snuff and knows the exact amount of fat in an avocado… but he looks like nothing. His numbers are pitiful. His midsection is soft and his chest sags. He makes excuses about why he isn't lifting more often than he actually lifts.

Much like the internet lifter, a lot of guys put the cart before the horse when it comes to starting a gang of men. They have all the info, the stats, the hypotheticals. And beyond that, they've got nothing beyond the dubious prestige of being a guy who is considered "pretty sharp" on some fucking internet forum, while they throw out the latest finds on "game" and "bro-science" before they jerk off to porn and go to bed after an unsatisfying night of video games or zombie movies.

If you want to Start the World, get ready to be uncomfortable. Get ready to get off your ass, off your computer, off your iPhone and out into the world that you're trying to change.

I'm about to hit you with a plan that isn't the product of debate, hypothesis, or something I read on the internet manosphere somewhere. It is the result of actual experience, real-world execution of the will, and a healthy dose of action over all. It is explained in brief, but in order. It works, and I know this, because it IS working. The Wolves of Vinland were crushing weights, throwing events, bareknuckle boxing, wearing back-patches, engaging in tribe-specific blood ritual and promoting the advancement of their own organically created culture from the get-go, going on seven years ago. We started a tribe not because we read about it on the internet, or because anyone told us it would be a "good idea." We did it because we NEEDED to do it, the same way every man needs to belong to a tribe of true peers in a meaningful fashion that pushes him upwards and onwards to better himself and his life. Here's how:

***Assemble a crew.*** This bit is obvious- without numbers, there is no group. The number can start small, but you will need at least 5 people or thereabouts to get anything done. There's been a lot said about how and where you can meet like-minded individuals, but I'd recommend starting out with a least a few guys that you've already known for a long time. Discuss your angle and your goals and get going with it. Don't waste a long time discussing direction or philosophy- that's the main point of this whole piece: no matter what, don't get caught up and dragged down in too much talking. Just start doing — the rest will work itself out and those discussions can be had when they're actually necessary. At the beginning, you just need to DO.

***Set your immediate goals immediately.*** Don't worry too much about "where you'd like to see the group in 5 years." This is bullshit, and will only lead to arguing, multiple directions and dissatisfaction. Instead, worry about what it is you want to achieve NOW, and go after it.

***Your initial goal is a location***. The driving force at the outset of any group should be to OWN your own place of meeting, hanging out, building, and recreation. A small building or house is a good goal, so is a garage for starters — but the main drive here is for space that is specifically used for only the "gang" — not a friend's basement or backyard. This defeats the purpose and is not a "group goal," because one guy's ld is not the gang's land. Buy property, either undeveloped or already built on and use it for tribal activity. Every successful crew has a place of their own. This is achieved through financial teamwork, which brings up the next point.

***Dues are mandatory***. Unfortunately, in this world of ours, nothing is for nothing. You need loot to work with, and this is where dues come in. Set the figure at an achievable level for the lowest earner in the group, or find a middle ground. Remember, at the beginning, this number has to be high enough to actually do something with — 5 guys pitching 10 bucks a month? Forget it. 5 guys pitching 100 a month, or even 50? Now you're able to get somewhere. In many states in this country, land goes for about 4,000 (some places more, some less) bucks an acre. If your take in dues is 500 a month, this means that a down payment can be hustled up in a few short months on an acre or two of property.

***Make more money***. This ain't the mafia — we aren't talking about loan-sharking, illicit gambling or dope sales. There are other ways to increase the capital that a group can take in. Once you have property, you have a pretty wide array of ways to make an extra buck if you're enterprising enough. Throw events, concerts, whatever. Door money from things like this can go straight towards land payment or rent on your structure, whatever you have. If you've decided to go in with the boys on a structure instead of undeveloped land, you can use that space to lift, personal train, hold workshops, shows, fighting or lifting competition events, whatever. Use your imagination and make sure that the things that you've put your hard-earned cash out there for can be used to get that money back — no one wants to be in the red, and tribe is about making life better and easier for those involved. With some intelligence and follow-through, you can be paying your own guys to work your own events. Everybody wins.

***Develop culture***. The reason for tribe is obvious — the indicators of tribe are not always so. What is it that you are? What do you produce? What is your reason for existence? These are things that develop along the way, and often times, do not always require an answer. To simply exist as a unit is an end in and of itself, without a loftier or more philosophical approach. To be in a tribe is a reason to have a tribe. However, there are many things that can be done to increase tribal pride, clout, identity and legend. These things are of course, up to each to decide for themselves and depend largely on the angle of the group, but can come in the form of shared language, identifying marks or worn items, group ritual, name-giving ceremonies, blood-oaths, and a thousand other things that give your tribe identity and worth to those within it.

*Hierarchy*. A good idea at some point is to work out who will perform what function within a group. It might seem to many like this is something that should be decided from the beginning, but experience has shown this to not be the case. Depending on what type of group you have, you might have absolutely no reason to name someone "Secretary" just because you read that you should have one. The person who you give this responsibility to at the start may be terribly unsuited for this position, or much better suited to perform another function. Hierarchy often works itself out with no need for titles, and this is often a much better way to work things. Like Fight Club, these things are pretty much a "choose your own level of involvement." Certainly, a great deal of things should be mandatory: dues, official "work-days," certain other commitments etc., but at the end of the day, there will always be a circle of people who are much more invested in the everyday running of the operation, and this group will often ebb and flow over a long period of time. This in itself is a pretty good reason not to worry too much about "official" jobs and titles — find someone who can and is willing to do the thing you need done and have them do it until such a time as you have to find someone else, if that arises. A point I will continue to keep hammering on is that the worst thing you can do in a tribal or group setting is waste time worrying or adding bureaucracy where it is not needed. This is the sort of thing that poisons a group, eliminates its fluidity and activity and replaces it with red-tape, too many rules and regulations and leads from action back to words again.

***Find out what is important to you by doing it excellently***. The main thing that will foster the growth of your group and lead to long term stability (an extremely rare thing) is to organically discover the things that you excel at and want to form the identity of your group around by doing them often, and well. Whatever it is that your group does, you should do your best to BE the best at it. This is obviously pretty "group specific," but it holds a lot of weight. There is no sense in doing anything as a group unless you are trying to make fucking legends. Why would you want to be anything else?

***Maintain order and stability by finding a positive way to work out disputes***. Probably the most important and absolutely necessary thing in a group is to find a way to keep arguments and in-fighting something that stimulates growth and productive action instead of tearing your tribe apart. This is done by setting protocol when it needs to be set by group consensus and then following it. If someone is fucking up, and you see them fucking up: deal with it immediately. Talk to them one on one and try to work it out on a small scale. If it continues, approach them with one or two other guys and have the conversation about it again. If that doesn't work, bring it to the tribe at large and sort it out there. In the event of an argument between members, bring them together for mediated discussion. Let them work it out man to man, only interrupting or mediating when it becomes necessary — encourage them to sort it out with words, then find out if violence is an appropriate answer — there are a lot of things that two guys will drop before having to fistfight. There are also plenty of things that a fistfight will sort out that words cannot. If neither of things work, hold counsel with all other members and decide who will stay and who will go. Schism in a group, if left to do its septic work, will rot an organization from the inside. Deal with things decisively and quickly before they become "a whole thing."

\*\*\*

Lastly, forming a tribe is difficult work. It is often times like an extremely complex marriage to someone with a horrible case of multiple personality disorder. It will require constant forward motion to survive. It will require mediation and problem solving and leadership and the ability to follow group consensus.

Any road worth walking is difficult and beset by hardship on all sides. The only question we need to ask ourselves, is will we get out there and Start the World, or will we watch it pass us by? When the great storm arises, the tribeless man is the lifeless man.

# XV.
# UNCONDITIONAL STRENGTH

TRANSMISSION DATE: 01-03-14

In this weak and saccharine world, we often hear terms like "love yourself unconditionally," "be okay with who you are," "find someone that loves you for you," and other such disgusting nonsense created by weak, sparrow-hearted types FOR weak, sparrow-hearted types.

These kind of greeting card sentiments are, of course, very popular in our culture that attempts to force this sort of all accepting, "all people are equal," "everyone must be praised the same" credo down the throats of those who are actually strong, or are becoming strong — people who know that the idea of equality is in opposition to natural law. People who know that one cannot simply "be okay" with weakness, failure, shortcoming or obstacle.

Possibly (but not definitely) with exception to parental love — "unconditional love" is for cunts. Unconditional love is not love at all, it is a surrender of strength — it is telling yourself or another person that you are a doormat, and will love them even if they treat you like garbage. Truly, there is no such thing as unconditional love, anyway, since there are always conditions on everything in this life, spoken or unspoken. The point is, why the hell would you want to love anything unconditionally? Those conditions are what keep us moving forward on a balanced playing field, keep us dissatisfied with our current level of progress, striving toward a higher state of being, to more personal power, and so on.

We should love our strengths under the condition that we grow them stronger. We should hate our weaknesses and seek their total eradication. We should consider ourselves a totalitarian dictator, with our qualities making up the populace of our tyrannical system — the strengths should be our inner cabinet, rewarded, encouraged to thrive and prosper. Our weaknesses should be herded onto cattle cars, isolated in awful little camps surrounded by barbed wire — and exterminated.

We should stop surrounding ourselves with people who want to pat us on the back and fellate us for every little meaningless thing, and instead surround ourselves with hardened individuals who accept no failure from us or themselves, people who inspire us to become stronger, even if it means imitating them until we no longer need to do so, as our daily struggle is to surpass them.

We should fight more, in every sense of the word — physically as well as metaphorically. If we want something, we must have the strength of character and the discipline to reach out and take it with a crushing grip. If we are put into a violent situation, we must be able to act equally or more violently than the other individuals involved, and we must be able to do so without fear or uncertainty.

We should remain MEN, in a world of irony, sarcasm and falsehood, one in which "males" are only really classified as such by their genitalia, understanding nothing of the iron and fire that it takes to be a man. We should sneer at emasculating trends, and speak out against them publicly, never concerning ourselves with our social standing in THEIR world, as it is crumbling, rotting from within, as weak and pitiful as the half-men who roll it blindly toward the cliff it must surely fall from. If we fear to speak from the heart publicly or in private, we have lost our part in the struggle and must hang our heads in shame, knowing that we will never stand for anything again.

We should rekindle the fires of the mannerbund, clanning together with like minds and strong wills, to add more mighty voices to our own, so that through the combined and unstoppable force of our Will, we can remake the world in the image we see fit. The only way forward is with Iron and Blood.

# XVI.
# BE WHO YOU SAY YOU ARE

TRANSMISSION DATE: 01-17-14

We are not who we say we are. Each one of us is guilty, at times, of letting the person we wish we were, or wish to be perceived as, overtake the reality of the real person underneath. It is an honorable life's work to constantly seek to make the person you are match up with the person you wish to be.

Words and talk, especially in this era of social media and internet communication can be a great obstacle to this Work — we look for immediate gratification or accolades from people (many or most of whom we don't even know) for deeds not yet undertaken, deeds talked about, deeds made weaker and less likely to occur the more we discuss them.

In the words of Odin, from the poem "Havamal," he says, "each word led me to another word, each deed to another deed." There is an important lesson that can be learned here: words, more often than not, lead to more words. A discussion seeds another discussion, and so on, until the participants are exhausted with discussion, tired of the initial idea, and bored by the entire concept that they've worked and overworked ad nauseam, without ever having accomplished anything tangible.

It is deeds that lead to more deeds. Personal power and individual might is built like a fire — a small spark strikes tinder, and a little flame is born from that spark. This is the flame of animus that a creature is given when it is quickened and comes to life. From that point, the fate of that fire is entirely dependent on how it is fed. If it is left untended, it will quickly gutter and go out, reducing itself to smoky coals that provide little in the way of heat and light, until they are finally extinguished forever. If, however, we begin to feed the fire with the fuel of deed, we see a progression: first, simple, achievable goals are set and manifested, twigs on the fire that will not smother the as yet meager flame — these the fire quickly eats, and the fire grows larger, can handle more fuel, bigger fuel, more challenging endeavors. If we continue in this fashion, there is no limit to the heights that our bonfire can reach, burning entire trees at once with our massive realized potential.

Talk is like blowing on coals without adding sticks for them to feed on. The coals will burn brightly for a moment, and then return to a dormant state, and this can only be done so many times before the fire is extinguished from the lack of available fuel. Words should be used to fan flames that are also being fed with mighty deeds. The by-words of the Fianna, those men of renown who fought and died under the likes of Finn MacCool, were: "Pure hearts. Strong limbs. Actions matching words." These seven words could be said to be what it really means to be a man.

In order for us to be who we say we are, we have to look at the truth that we are not what we SAY we are. We are what we DO. Who are you now, and who do you wish to become? What are you willing to sacrifice to get there? Words will only lead to more, but with action being our watchword, and success being our only proof, to what heights can we raise ourselves? There will come a time (if we live wildly and ferociously, adventurously, there will be many such times), where we will be forced to live up to the words we have spoken, to offer proof of our statements, whether they be truth or hubris. Live your lives in such a way that you are always prepared to offer proof of a statement, to risk life and limb to demonstrate that you in fact can be what you say you are, as long as you are doing what you say you do. Walk your talk, and let your deeds be praised more often by others than by yourself.

# XVII.
# THE DUTY OF A HERO

TRANSMISSION DATE: 02-05-2014

Under a spell of deep slumber, the vast populace of Empire lies dreaming. The dream, however, is cracking at the edges, and through each fracture leaks a profound and unshakeable discontent. Discontent, uncertainty, the distinct feeling of enslavement — and anger.

The dream-weavers of Empire create a wondrous woven tapestry of transitory pleasures, the thousand glittering lights of their illusion, each one a different solar system revolving around a great and burning lie: that any man or woman's dreams can be created for them, instead of by them.

Far away from the wretched hovels and muddy streets, the concrete walls, the broken lives and hidden knives that strike in the dark, around marbled tables holding maps crafted from human hide, the Everlasting Council of the Undying Ones convenes. Their ancient rituals of domination and perpetuation have been set since the forgotten dawn of Empire — carefully wrought strategies of control and command, each word they speak spiraling outward to the farthest reaches of their Imperium, these god-kings enthroned on the twin pillars of uncontrollable avarice and never-ending war.

In the small surviving woodlands at the very edges of Empire, other councils are meeting. Savages, barbarians, those tribal leaders who have risen up from the filth and squalor that was their birthright, making of themselves mighty men of renown, reavers and outlaws, warlords whose entire life-stories have been written in blood.

They have not looked to a distant future for the ideal time to congregate and unite themselves under a common banner; nor have they shrugged off the responsibility, leaving it to their children, or their children's children to cast off the shackles of Empire, those chains made of generations of complacency and servitude — chains made of dominion through horror, fear, violence and forced poverty.

These men are not scholars, nor philosophers. They have not pontificated and debated over leather bound tomes regarding the positive nature of revolt, of freedom, of a life lived with no masters. They simply know in their bones that this was not the life that was meant for them, and their anger smolders within them, unquenchable with anything save the gore running freely from the throats of every king of every nation.

Their oath has been made to one another. Their tribes have pledged brotherhood under common cause- to see the rulers and tyrants of this world gasp out their last while clawing uselessly at spilling entrails, a boot on their throat, scalp removed from skull and hung from the battle-standards of a hundred tribes.

The chieftains of these tribes bear a great and terrible weight of responsibility. They cannot wait for the certainty of victory — for there is no such certainty. Every year they wait, saying "just a little longer, now," they grow older, the fire of their spirit burns a little less brightly, limbs grow weaker, hearts less firm in their resolve, homes more comfortable. They know that a time will not come in their lifetime that will make this battle easier, so they prepare themselves daily for the war they will soon wage.

They lift stones the size of foothills, use the very fallen trees of the forest to make their bodies harder than steel. They run like wild wolves through the woodlands of their ancestral homes, making war on their rivals with fire, iron, lead and fist — training their bodies and minds in the ancient ways of brutal combat, knowing that when the time comes to hurl themselves past the enemies spear-wall, they will be ready.

They swell the numbers of their tribes with solitary warriors, braves from amongst the ruins on the outskirts of Empire, those who have seen the strength of the old tribal ways and look to become counted among their ranks — these untested men swear oaths of loyalty to their new brethren in blood and ash out beneath the stars, where trees as old as Empire itself look down in silent approval.

In the dancing firelight, rituals of equinox and solstice — these tribes are tied to the land and sky, to blood and old god, sacrificial offerings stain the stone altars black beneath the waning moon and these tribes come together to howl beneath it, calling their far-away kinsmen to join with them in their war against the horror and desolation of Empire.

They cannot hope to win alone, and perhaps, they cannot hope to win at all. But they will prepare themselves for the fight nonetheless — because this, since time immemorial, has been the duty of the hero.

# XVIII.
# SONS OF PERDITION

TRANSMISSION DATE: 02-12-2014

This age calls for complete men. Warriors who are not simply specialists, focusing only on the function of their martial abilities or physical regimen, but possessed of a certain mental and spiritual faculty that allows them to see beyond; to be aware of the emptiness and the hollowness of this age in which we live, and to be able to shatter its façade like the blow of a hammer to glass.

There exist only two classes in this world — the wealthy and the slave. We must once again create the warrior caste, the illumined knight of old, the transcendent berserker, wolf-masked and war-ready, immersed in the lore and ritual of the primal death cults, while still ably treading the filthy roads of modernity; a savage, a guerilla soldier entrenched behind enemy lines with the single-minded goal of self-transformation and constant, merciless violence against the illusion and lie of Progress.

Operation: Werewolf is merely doorway, an in-road to this new warrior caste, an esoteric order of Knights, men who have chosen to free themselves from the inevitable path toward self-destruction that the Iron Age has placed them on; men who have no choice in life but to seek the heights of something greater than they have been offered by this banal world of mindless toil and useless striving toward artificial goals; men whose hearts have been gripped by the Need to become whole, living archetypes.

In order to achieve this, we must have a plan — an Operations Manual that we can follow, in the knowledge that there are others of our Order who are following this path as we are, undergoing these solitary trials and ordeals on the road to Knighthood, with an undying light in their eyes and blood in their mouths- so that one day soon, we will meet in the flesh and start the fire that will burn away the great rotten constructs of this age, and from those ashes- growth, wholesome and green.

We must condition ourselves to face hardships physical, mental and spiritual. We will set ourselves on a path of supremacy that requires the deepest commitment and conviction — fanatical, we will apply ourselves to overcoming the dross within. Knowing that we are both hammer and anvil, as well as the raw material upon it, we will re-forge what this world has broken, and once again be made whole through dedication to ancient, non-transitory principles that have held true since the dawn of man.

Slowly, we will assume the form desired. We will destroy the influence of modernity on us through the love of Truth. We will unify the false dichotomies through the yoga of Action and Experience. We will make of our flesh a temple. We will make of our mind a weapon.

We will make of our spirits a pure fire, without smoke. We will make of this world a cremation ground from which shall spring the new dawn: the Age of the Hero.

# XIV.
# COME FORTH

TRANSMISSION DATE: 02-15-2014

If you have looked around yourself and seen the world for the empty husk it truly is, and you have desired more; if you have an unquenchable lust for real adventure and overcoming in an age where the word HERO has become meaningless; if you would make an outlaw of yourself, and go against everything that this Kali Yuga represents — then come to the blazing council fires, join us and raise our standard high, or come bearing your own, it is of small importance...what is of great importance is that we begin to band together, wanderers and lone-wolves, chieftains and tribesmen from all corners of Empire, uniting for common cause.

Lurkers in the shadow, come forth! Solitary for so long that you have forgotten the meaning of true fellowship with minds sharp as your own, those who rage against the tide of decay, wrapping themselves in the impenetrable armor of truth and a great and righteous hatred for the filth of the Iron Age.

Cease your time in hiding and declare allegiance — now is the time for you to live up to your words of strength and elitism, spoken loudly and often from the comforts of home- riding, they say, is easy for every man while he sits in the hall.

Tribal leaders, come forth! You who have built a clan out of the ashes of tradition, sworn oaths and brotherhood, but have no greater cause — is it not now time to change the world? Have we become so weary that we no longer feel the surge of possibility in our hearts as we did when we were younger men? Put on your battle-dress and paint your faces with symbols of war! The moment is at hand when we must realize that our grievances and differences can wait to be settled another day, but for now, we must ride together toward a common destination, a common enemy.

In the east, and in the west, the Wolf-head stands white on a field of black, a symbol of pure fury calling forth those who are up to the challenge. In the streets of Empire, and at its decaying edges, the songs of destruction and new growth are being howled from throats that had once borne the collar of civilization — no longer! From the Great Plains to the Eastern Forest of that land called Vinland, men and women bear the standard that reads WOLVES, spattered with the blood of sacrifice, stained with the ash of the ritual fire-that banner is worn on our backs, so that any who see it and wish to rally to that cause may undergo the trials required to roar savagely at the world: "I was a man, but now I have become a wolf!"

Through trial and ordeal, through rage and ruin, through fierce love and the fire of Will — we will overcome.

# XV.
# USE YOUR FUCKING HEAD

## Magical Techniques for Strength, Part One

TRANSMISSION DATE: 04-24-14

Anyone who maintains the standpoint that lifting weights is not a very cerebral approach is probably doing it wrong, and I'm not talking here about nutritional science, programming the perfect block periodization or trying to understand the back of your supplement containers.

Anyone who moves heavy weight will tell you that visualization, mental focus and proper mindset are three very important factors for a successful lifting session, and that a lack of any of these things can be a major obstacle between being one of those guys who fucks around in the gym and never sees real results or lifting like a wild animal and hitting the numbers you want.

In theory, controlled visualization works in the following fashion: you envision yourself already having accomplished a thing, so that when the time comes to actually do it, you've fooled yourself into thinking that you've already overcome that challenge, thereby making it easier to "repeat."

In practice, it demands extreme focus and clarity, and has allowed me to destroy PRs by creating the experience so thoroughly and realistically in my mind that I was sure I had already done it. When you apply this technique (I usually do it in a quiet spot, the night before I plan to accomplish whatever it is I am visualizing), take your time and really invest yourself in the reality you 池 e creating. Put on some favorite lifting music to make the connection.

Start slow, perhaps approaching your gym or weight room, seeing the area as it truly is, the look, sound, smell and feel of the place. Look down at your hands in your mind's eye, see your tattoos, your scars, defining marks.

Approach the bar, feel the roughness of the knurling in your grip, set it in place and load the weights on- one plate at a time, counting up toward your goal, hearing that clang of the iron slapping together.

Ready yourself for the lift. Get into position, and move the weight — this is the important bit. Feel it in your muscle fibers, that hard strain, but know that you've got it. Just like real life, that overwhelming surge of force as you crush your way through the sticking point and realize that you're going to complete the motion, and then lock it out. You're done. You've hit it. Fix that feeling, that whole scenario in your mind as objectively real, a thing that has already been accomplished. If you've done it properly, when you go to hit it "for real," it's like you're hitting a lift that you know you did last week.

Staying focused on the task at hand is another essential. It can be tempting to allow yourself to break out of "the zone" after each completed set, to bullshit with your training partner about your day, to check your texts, whatever. Resist the urge.

Every time you break focus on what you're doing, your brain goes back to its day to day function- it turns off "animal mode" and allows you to communicate with other humans without baring your teeth and growling, or perform normal activities without going berserk. This is not what you want when you are moving weight. Your goal is to hit a point of mental savagery so pure that communicating in anything other than roars and grunts is not possible, your eyes bloodshot and frenzied, every muscle ready to rend and tear and heave.

Once you've attained that berserker rage, hold onto it — it'll help you hit your lifts, and raise your testosterone in the process. Your rest time will be shorter, as you'll be barely able to contain yourself from attacking the weights again and again, which will keep your heart rate elevated and drastically improve the cardiovascular benefit of your lifting session. Your mind will stay on the enemy, and it will overcome.

Coming into a workout with the proper mindset is imperative. I can't count the amount of times I've heard people struggling to edge out another last rep saying, "I can't, I can't" to their partner, as their limbs slowly follow their words and fail out on the lift. Well of course you fucking can't. Words have power, and when we say things like this, we are putting into motion a spell of weakness and failure. The same goes for walking into the gym and saying to a friend, "I feel weak today." Well, now you are even weaker. You've given voice to a potential, and now it has form: you.

Banish these thoughts from your mind, attack the weights with ferocity, do not allow yourself to be brought down into the morass of mediocrity or a conquered mindset — only conquer. Become strength itself. Create mantras for yourself and repeat them while you do the work, ensorcelling your limbs with the craft of power, of might, of overcoming.

If someone you train with likes to talk a lot, wear headphones. If they are negative, tell them to stay the fuck home — you'd rather lift yourself. If you've had a shitty day, bring it with you to the gym, but bring it in the right way - to destroy it by using it to power your machine, not by allowing it to defeat you or sap the strength from your blood. This is a discipline for conquerors only — so set about conquering, or prepare to be conquered.

# XVI.
# LIFT WHAT THOU WILT

## Magical techniques for Strength,
## Part Two

TRANSMISSION DATE: 05-02-2014

The famous magician Aleister Crowley defined magick as: "the Science and Art of causing Change to occur in conformity with Will," He went on to state that: "*Magick is the Science of understanding oneself and one's conditions. It is the Art of applying that understanding in action.*"

If one replaces the term "magick" with "strength training or bodybuilding," they will see it as perfectly applicable. As stated in the first part of this series, we know that weightlifting is not an entirely physical process, but a mental one as well — here, we will go further by stating that it is a blend of the mental, the physical, and the divinely spiritual, as man seeks to make of himself a god by elevating that triad to the highest form he is able.

To do this, he must learn to act in tandem with his Will, that is, the goals he has chosen to achieve must be like the unfailing light of the North star — his gaze must be solely fixed on its piercing light, and all distraction and illusion must be cast aside.

*"One must find out for oneself, and make sure beyond doubt, who one is, what one is, why one is... Being thus conscious of the proper course to pursue, the next thing is to understand the conditions necessary to following it out. After that, one must eliminate from oneself every element alien or hostile to success, and develop those parts of oneself which are specially needed to control the aforesaid conditions."*

Inconsistency, lack of dedication to a chosen goal, a spirit easily broken, and compromising ones' initial plans are diseases that plague the world, and this is especially true in the gym. I have heard, *ad nauseam*, individuals laud their newly chosen program, their new diet, their new split, whatever, raising it up on a pedestal of perfection, praising the massive gains they have seen through its application, and exhorting you to come over to their side of things, where the grass is green as a shining emerald... for a few weeks. Then, invariably, they become frustrated with early plateau, gains are not coming as fast as they'd like anymore, the workouts are too hard or too easy, "things just aren't working anymore."

Here is a statement you can hold close to your heart as a perfect truth in the world of strength training: If you lift heavy weight, and eat a lot of (good) food, you will grow in size and become stronger. This is a fact. It is not a secret. Every single new program you find that stirs a fire in your whorish loins where your last one has left you flaccid and listless, will follow this exact same idea, in some form or another, although they will invariably tout themselves as being superior to every other nearly identical one out there.

After realizing this, one must come to the realization: The main obstacle between you and your goals is you. It is your weakness, your impatience, your petulance, your negative bullshit attitude — if you think that you will attain your goals in short order with little effort and few pitfalls on the way, not only are your goals pitiful and not worth obtaining, but you are a weak cunt who has no business on the Road of Heroes. Your goal should simply be to place one foot in front of the other on that Road, and never cease until your last ragged breath — that is a fucking goal worth attempting!

Your constant setting of specific goals and expectations of "where you should be" will generally lead to demoralization and a lowering of zeal, whereas, if one's goal is to simply continue to become stronger, day after day, week after week, year after year, he will simply lower his horns like the aurochs signified in the URUZ rune and bellow a challenge at himself and the world around him, advancing step by endless step — unstoppable, unshakeable, unbroken.

The point is to seize every occasion of bringing every available force to bear upon the objective of the assault. It does not matter what the force is (by any standard of judgment) so long as it plays its proper part in securing the success of the general purpose [...] We must constantly examine ourselves, and assure ourselves that every action is really subservient to the One Purpose.

Our lives must become this Great Work. Al of our energy must be honed and directed towards becoming and being Strong. Mentally. Spiritually. Physically.

If something is not working in our lives, it must be examined closely, and if one determines that this is a thing not aiding us in our war against the mundane, it must be immolated completely — burned out of existence, no longer digging its hooks into us and sapping us of the vitality that we desperately need to achieve the art of unrestrained action.

If we can do this honestly and unmercifully, we then have some hope of one day cresting that mountaintop in the full realization of what we have set out to accomplish: *"...ultimately the change will be complete; God manifest in flesh will be his name."*

# XVII.
# FROM PUTRIFICATION
# TO PURIFICATION

## Magical Techniques for Strength,
## Part Three

TRANSMISSION DATE: 07-17-14

There are times when even the strongest fall prey to one of the thousand lights of illusion that flicker throughout this world of despair and distraction, and are led astray from the Road of Heroes, their footsteps faltering into the disease riddled whorehouse of modern culture. Its poisons and debasements at times can appear irresistible, infinitely easier and more comforting than the lifestyle we have chosen for ourselves — one of steel and Truth, might and myth- and we succumb to its paralyzing venom.

Like one in a stupor, we wander aimlessly, intoxicated by the feeling of freedom and wantonness that is initially felt when we turn our back on the heavy weight of duty and self-sacrifice; drunk on our new-found liberation, we stagger from sense pleasure to sense pleasure, overloading ourselves with saccharine experience. We hail libertinage and hedonism, sagely declaring that one should not deprive themselves of life's many enjoyments, and for a time, we even believe ourselves.

After a honeymoon phase with the bride known as Indulgence, we realize that she is pox-ridden, and what began as pleasure and joyous gratification has become a sickness that grows within us, and its only cure is a prescription written for more and more. We begin to satisfy every urge that strikes our fancy, from drink, to drug, to simple sloth, and our Will, once a roaring flame that consumed weakness within its mighty flame, has died into ashes with barely an ember remaining. Our flesh grows weak, our minds fogged with a haze of burn-out and self-disgust as we watch the empire we have built crumbling around us, our bodies now a prison that we no longer hold the key to.

But this low point is not the end — rather, it is the beginning of a road to redeeming ourselves through the twin pillars of Strength and Purification. The knowledge must come that indulgence for its own sake can bring no true pleasure to the man of power — only transitory distraction from duty and honor. The hero understands that he was meant for something far greater than a life lived for cheap thrill and delirium, and that his only real satisfaction must come through an existence defined by the overcoming of great obstacles — of fearsome acts that grow his own personal myth, of realizing his higher destiny of becoming an archetype of awe and supremacy. This is his duty then: to himself, to his own strength of arm, will and spirit- to inspire those around him to :K:eep :R:ising with a constant display of unshakeable, brutal defiance of his own weaknesses.

The world around him becomes not anathema, but proving ground — he transcends its pitfalls and snares through ritual purification at the altar of Blood and Iron. The fire within him awakens again, and roars to new heights, fed with all the dross of his transgressions against strength. It burns clear and clean, without smoke, its light seen for great distances — it lights new fires around itself, which in turn become great in their own right, and combined, they burns the filth of the world away and make clean the earth.

# XVIII.
# ON MAGIC

TRANSMISSION DATE: 07-21-14

*An article I'd written several years ago and lost along the way, recently sent to me by someone who enjoyed it. A bit dated, but much of it still rings true for me.*

I have felt compelled to write this brief explanation of my theories and belief based around questions, arguments, conversations and even accusations that have been brought to me over the past several months. I would like to preface this by stating that the following is completely personal opinion, and does not represent the official views of any of the groups that I may be affiliated with. I am also not putting forth the idea that I am an "expert" on this topic, nor that my opinions and experiences are more or less "correct" than anyone else...this is the nature of the subject at hand. I have been an extremely active student of the occult sciences for most of my life, beginning my studies of runework and basic magic principle and practice around the age of 9 years old, and have studied numerous traditions in several organizations over the course of my life. After becoming a heathen in my teenage years, I left any focus on other traditions for a strictly Northern approach, working as holistically within this framework as possible, while at the same time trying to develop further down the pathway of self-transformation set down for us through the example of Odinn. The following is an attempt to put forth my explanation to as many of the questions and arguments as possible.

To begin, the necessary question is first: What is magic? Many of the people I have talked to about this topic come into the conversation with an aggressive standpoint, making it clear to me that they "do not believe in magic," and that they are expecting me to prove its existence to them by performing some sort of awe-inspiring act of pure sorcery. My first rebuttal to this is to simply ask them what they mean specifically that they do not believe in, and that perhaps their perception and my perception of what magic truly is may be a bit different.

Defined in the most basic of terms, magic is one's Will being consciously employed to make change in reality: both subjectively and objectively. This is a pretty vague understanding of so complex a topic. What exactly do we mean here when we say "employing the will," or "changing reality?" Truly, the will is needed in order for a human to perform any action, no matter how insignificant. The difference here is that we are talking about a conscious usage of this personal power to enact a change on a level that goes beyond the insignificant, and truly re-shapes this reality we exist in…not simply exerting the everyday willpower needed to go check the mail, or walk the dog- although this of course changes the world in some way as well.

The accumulation of this sort of personal power is an idea that consumes a great deal of the vitki's time and life, like any true art form — time is needed to develop the necessary skills, technique, knowledge, understanding and application of this thing, and the first step along this road is understanding what magic is and what it is not.

For many people, their understanding of the very idea of "magic" has been shaped by stage-tricks, fantasy novels, television shows and the like. The word to them represents a childish belief, evoking images of cartoon mice with magic wands or old men in pointy hats prodding short, pointy-eared folks into trilogies. The word has essentially been hi-jacked away from its true meaning, and now only implies something that is a shadow of the original understanding of it. An easier understanding of this would be to look at what has happened to the English word "gay." Generally when this is being said, it has no connection with the idea of being upbeat — the word's meaning has changed, and our understanding of it has likewise changed along with the misappropriation.

This is an unfortunate road-block when discussing the subject with most people, and effort has to be spent to break their perceptions, so that they don't think you are suggesting that a vitki can turn someone into a newt. The struggle is made much more difficult by many modern day "witches," who spend a great deal of time re-enforcing these absurd stereotypes, waving crystals around and touting spells to turn your boyfriend into a love-slave, or some other such ridiculous nonsense.

When I say magic, I mean something much different, and much more powerful than all this self-delusional bullshit. If you're looking to make traffic lights change for you/magically get a raise at work/seduce your boss/improve your sex life/whatever, seek out your local Barnes and Noble, head to the New Age section, and pick out any number of amazing and intelligent books by authors with names like Silvershine RavenMoon WolfSongbird and join a Wiccan coven... I'm sure your wildest dreams will come true.

True magic, however, is self-sacrifice. It is a fanatical devotion to self-transformation and self-improvement: learning, acting and growing. The real power of magic lies in its ability to change one's subjective universe — his perception of reality, his interaction with both physical and numinous energy and so forth, and that in so doing, the objective universe molds to that change.

The runes, and the arts of galdr, seidhr, and other specific disciplines found within the Northern Tradition are the tools of our trade, and are used in tandem with one's will or as a focal point to effect this change. One can shake the very foundations of the Nine Worlds with this craft, but in order to do so, he must constantly grow and change his own structure, adapting to new situation and experience, and using the past as a great well of might to shape his present, and sow seeds for his future.

So, as far as this argument is concerned, I don't believe in "magic," either, at least not the kind these people are talking about.

Now that we have touched briefly on what magic isn't, and what it is on a very basic level, it comes time to define a bit further. 1) How are these processes enacted? 2) What must one do in order to use, or tap into this deep ocean? 3) What can magic be used for, and how does it work?

Magic "works", by a vitki summoning his Will, the numinous energy that drives our existence, and using that force in a very direct and focused way — deciding what his Need is, and how to overcome those obstacles through the usage of these aforementioned tools...leaving him with the simple question of "what you would change, and WHY." (quote taken from Gandvaldr Bláskikkja.)

Many people have passed this off as a subjective psychological tool, as though that made it somehow less powerful or less impressive. In truth, there is a great deal of psychological benefit from these techniques, and a great many of these techniques are, indeed, psychological ones. What, do you suppose, were psychologists called before we had fancy scientific words for everything? This is not to say that the entire process is a psychological one. No, something very definite happens on a realm well outside that which is generally termed "physical reality." Change occurs. Creation occurs. Destruction occurs, and everything within the complex of reality is changed because of this, in many ways, and for many reasons.

The constant argument to this is always: "This is not real. It is merely a self-delusional process that occurs within the person's psyche, and they force themselves into thinking that they have affected something with their mind." An argument, by the way, that has led to psychologists claiming that the idea that one can affect change in the world based around his mental capacity or Will is a sign of schizophrenia.

The rebuttal to this is: What is reality, and isn't all reality in truth, subjective? Aleister Crowley's argument against this was to bring up the example of "love". Love, he said, was a chemical response in the brain that released dopamine and other such lovely components, and made one feel a certain way about someone. This is scientific fact. Hate, itself, is the same thing...a chemical reaction producing extreme feelings of aggression, anger and so forth. Now, we cannot "see" love, nor hate, nor any other emotion. We can only see the product of it made manifest on a physical plane. Does this mean that love and hate are not real, because they exist within a person's "subjective" reality, and we can only see their manifestation? Of course not. On the same hand, if one works a ritual and sings galdr with the intent and focus behind it to destroy his enslavement to some substance or another, and if after the working, his addiction is gone- is the ritual just a hoax? Or are we seeing a powerful manifestation of true power worked on a spiritual scale? The answer to the rational mind is obvious.

The second question, relating to the idea of what one must do in order to use these processes: He must turn his life into a living rune, an absolute representation of Will, dedication and discipline. If one hasn't the time on his hands to dedicate his life to this art, then he has no business in it whatsoever. I have often heard the sentence, "I practice rune-work in my spare time." The complete laughability of this statement says worlds about the lack of seriousness with which most approach this subject, even when it comes to "believers." An equal amount of people have told me that they used to "do magic," but that they stopped "doing" it after a few months, because it "didn't work." This would be like deciding you wanted to be a body-builder, or UFC fighter, or some other life-demanding pursuit that in order to master, one must give their entire world over to — and then lifting weights once a month, eating like shit, occasionally taking a couple swings at a heavy bag, and having the audacity to say that your training "didn't work," because you are not a champion. In the first case, these are people going back to this idea that magic somehow "works" for you, an animate object, that you only need to say the "power words" for, and "hey-presto!" a black cat appears to accompany you to the coffee-shop. Or what-have-you.

In order to be a vitki, there can be no other pursuits. One may be and do many things in his life as a vitki, but all these secondary things are just that: secondary. He must dedicate himself to long years of study, practice, frustration, confusion, failure, craftsmanship and finally Understanding — which at some points may be the hardest bit of all. No one can just tell you overnight how these things are done, because they did not learn overnight- besides which, if one isn't willing to put in the time, and just want the "magic words" told to them... even if it could be done, they would lack the necessary Will to use it.

This has to be built up over these long years of trial and error. But the first thing one Needs to do in order to begin unlocking these mysteries is simply desire it. After this initial flame is kindled, it is up to the aspiring vitki as to whether or not he has the massive fortitude to remain on the narrow road.

Finally, when dealing with the question of, "OK, so if it is real, and it takes these years and years and years to study and understand, what is the good of all of it?" In short, what can it be used for? This is the easiest question to deal with so far.

The simplest answer is: everything. Once one has absorbed the knowledge of the Work, and has understood that knowledge to a point where he can utilize it — it never stops being utilized. It becomes another faculty, as natural as seeing... its use is limitless and constant; direct and flowing. It makes itself manifest in the Word, the Deed, and the Thought. It wraps the being in itself, and its nature is as simple and wondrous as our own...we are meant for great things, and have stunted our spiritual capabilities for years upon years. This art exists to gain back that flame of Breath that is meant to burn within us: the only gift the gods ever gave freely — would we squander it, or rediscover it, and use it to live lives of True power, True understanding, and True wholeness?

# XIX.
# WOLVES TAKE
# WHAT WOLVES WILL

## By: Galdr, WoV

TRANSMISSION DATE: 08-01-14

In the cave-like dark of a hill-riven oak and poplar forest, twin fires snap and spark to the symphony of drone and growl, illuminating the feral ash-marked forms of men and women lost to time. Mani glides through the welkin, his faced turned from the under-life of the city not far distant, his attention snared by the deep chant of drum, the flash of steel, the scent of blood spilled on hot stone. Myriad pools of flame gleam in that darkness; the anger-laden eyes of men and women who would destroy a world, remorseless and laughing.

Those eyes which gleam in that darkness are devoid of hope, for hope, like faith, is an expectation unvetted by evidence — a child's folly. Those eyes are lit with determination, not hope; they are the outward corona of action-weighted spirit, not the meek flicker of wish and prayer. These men and women — these Wolves — have gathered not for obsecration; they are about in the night on an errand which Volund would smile upon. They seek not reconciliation, but revenge.

They turn, with sneering laughter, from the weak and unfit who would claim kinship with them. What palsied sheep can truly claim kinship with the slavering Wolf? They heap derision and shame upon the milling, tunic-wrapped flock of heathenry with its pork-belly faith, cumbrous with desert moralities. Let them gather in their impotent masturbatory pubmoots; the songs chanted in the unsketched future will be songs of Wolves, not sheep and swine.

Four of their number seperate from the rest, abide awhile at the cardinal points of the world. Rage-roughened voices echo through the benighted forest, calling numinous spears, braced ever outward. The very air reverberates with the power of their howls, the stamp of their bare feet shakes the earth of this forest which has glutted on so much of their blood and sweat. The scent of the gathered pack changes suddenly —from quiet expectation to rampant ecstasy— as Odin walks among them, driving frenzy-spikes deep into heart and mind.

The four speak, some with quiet insistence, others with od-tinged madness. The pack listens, still as stone statues of the Gods that they are. Other eyes now shine in the darkness, approving eyes of world-spectres and grave-kin, cheering silently for the cleansing blaze ignited by this Folk. The pack grows restless for the time for words has nearly ended; the days of knives wetted in the putrescent blood of a dying world is upon them.

A blood-spattered measure of mead is lifted to the pure, cold light of Mani; power snaps and swirls as these gore-maddened woods-witches sing ancient mysteries to the night; mysteries of blood and Tribe and bund. The sorceries growled by these vitkar snake into all gathered, wrap tight around their hearts, strangling weakness in its crib.

These Wolves will spread like fire across Midgard. They will burn a world and eat the ash; replanting a strong and vital world with each word, each deed, each conflagration ignited. They will make a world of iron-toothed Wolves, and they do not require blessings. They have decided — rightfully — that this world belongs to them, not the sheep-hearted bleaters that plague it today.

Wolves take what Wolves will.

# XX.
# BARBARIANS

TRANSMISSION DATE: 09-10-14

We cannot become content to watch other men and women live lives and perform actions that we feebly wish for ourselves, standing on the sidelines of the Great War of life, allowing others to break open the bones of mighty deeds and draw out the marrow of glory while we starve on the dust of mediocrity.

We must become heroes, barbarians of a new dawn — capable of great thought as well as great violence, intelligent savages able to express ourselves both mentally and physically with equal success. Our bodies should be a shrine to what we value, reflecting our inner values of strength and purity, displaying to the world that paganism, barbarism, is vital and strong with our very flesh.

Our minds must continue to be sharp as well, and our senses undulled with too much comfort, entertainment and idleness. We should seek out situations that make us uncomfortable, in order to discover our weaknesses and annihilate them.

Violence will never go out of style, and we will never live in a world where a man can be sure to avoid it — so we must prepare for it. In order to be heroes, we must earn that title through hardship and ordeal, deed and glory.

# XXI.
# PORN AND FOOTBALL

TRANSMISSION DATE 02-02-15

Millions of people right now are glued to a screen watching their fantasies play out in front of them; toned, muscled bodies on camera performing just for them — sweating and grunting with exertion. The viewers are totally invested in the action, waiting with baited breath, their sweaty hands moist with anticipation of the main star making penetration... into the endzone.

This similarity between professional sports and porn does not end there — both take in billions of dollars each year, both create celebrity status for their participants which they use to market product, and both contribute to a sickness that is weakening (predominantly) males across the world. That sickness is mediation.

With sports, this is seen even in the language fans use to refer to their chosen team — "we," "us," words of identity, grouping themselves in with a team of humans they have never, and likely will never meet, who they roar support for in the coliseum, wear jerseys branded with their favorite players name and number, and debate endlessly with other fans about how good "our program is this year." Sports fans participate in trivia nights at their local bars, citing endless statistic and minutiae — here's a statistic:

studies show that self-identifying sports fans are on average more unhealthy and in worse shape than those who are not.

The answer for this? Mediation. So much time spent sitting and watching others perform leads to a lack of desire to perform oneself. So too, with pornography — statistically, habitual pornography users are more likely to experience sexual dysfunction like ED, and have less grey matter in the brain areas related to sexual stimulation — like any drug, its continued use demands more and higher types of stimulation in order to achieve the same levels of interest.

Observation instead of participation is the name of the game in the modern world. Video games, sports, pornography, movies, reality television, even the news — it all leads systematically to becoming a "receiver" instead of a "sender," which is, of course, what the leaders of Empire have in mind for you. If your switch is constantly set to "receive," your brain becomes open, malleable, like a spongy mush ready to mop up and dribble out every bit of sewage they spew into it, a fucking invertebrate fit only for couch-ridden outbursts of approval or dismay at "your" team's escapades, "your" representative's political decisions, or to weakly leak out your pathetic seed as you savage yourself to another false representation of sexual contact between two slabs of painted meat slamming their surgically altered bodies together in feigned ecstasy.

This is not the life we were meant for: to wither or bloat like drowned corpses as the overminds dangle pretty distractions in front of our milky eyes, working for our whip-holders for a pitiful wage or a massive sum, either way to be spent on frivolous trinket or bourgeois comforts. We were meant to bite that hand that seeks to distract us! To tear free of that leash of mediation and docility, to rend the throats of those who would keep us in thrall!

Next time you sit down to play-off or jerk-off- consider what that time might be better spent doing — are you content to live in the cage that they've constructed for you, or would you rather bed down tonight after a real fight and a real fuck, with blood in your mouth, rebellion in your mind, and glory in your heart?

# XXII.
# TYRANT AND THRALL

TRANSMISSION DATE: 03-11-15

Within all of us, a constant war of the will is raging between our tyrant mind and our thrall mind. Each day we wake up, the servant attempts to resist his master with petulant cries and stubbornness, insubordination to the orders of that strong overlord who would make gods of us mere men.

It is this thrall mind that is our greatest opponent on the road to ascension. At times we will find ourselves completely siding with the slave aspect, and we wil know it when thoughts or words arise within us that we know to be weak — "I can't." "I don't feel like it." "It's too difficult."

We will use these as our mantra as we squander our hours in idle chatter, idle activity, bored indolence, as in the back our consciousness, the tyrant struggles to regain control.

The tyrant mind is a hard master, because he does not encourage or cajole — he only demands. He does not say "you can." He roars, "you will!" He does not comfort with "good try." He drives one onward with the lash of "not enough!"

The thrall mind will tell us that we have done enough for the day, that we are "above average," or that we deserve a break — the tyrant mind knows that we can do more, that our average is compared to peasants, not heroes, and that breaks and leisure are for those who are disinterested in becoming immortal.

We must become more and more the willing thrall of our own tyrant mind, until the slave and the master become one — the dichotomy is destroyed, and there is only the hero in its place.

# XXIII.
# WEAKNESS AND STRENGTH

TRANSMISSION DATE: 03-15-15

You are weak. Whether you have made a conscious decision to be weak, or because you are lazy, or because you are afraid of hardship — you are weak. You do not like being weak. You do not like being weak because no man likes being weak — it is part of our evolutionary nature to become strong, to desire strength, to admire strength, to obtain strength through mastery over the flesh. Your desire for strength has taken a distant last place in your list of many, many desires — most of them unobtainable for you, because you lack the Will to apply yourself to reach out with a scarred, brutal hand and grasp them in a crushing and iron-like grip.

Your spurned desire has turned into the bitterness of jealousy and envy, and in your jealousy and your envy you turn to the last bastion of the feeble: you mock the thing that you hate yourself for not being. Your mockery is hollow, and grates on your ears, and in the quiet hours of solitude, you yearn to be strong, and to be seen as strong.

Strength is admired for its own sake because it is difficult to obtain — certainly, some are born with more physical prowess than others, but through hard work and self-discipline, nearly anyone can make themselves powerful in physique, sculpted, pleasing to look upon, able to perform great feats of might... nearly anyone CAN, but a tiny few WILL.

This is because the average and the mediocre fear hardship and ordeal — a great terror surges up in them at the thought of breaking their habits, tearing down their idols to Laziness and Comfort and placing in their stead Iron and Blood.

We who lift and seek to become strong do so because it fills us with Pride.

Pride at the hours of grinding teeth, straining muscle and tendon, roaring exertion, blood rushing in our ears as we seek to simply move an object one more time.

Pride in our ability to continue to do a thing that is physically painful, mentally challenging, time consuming and at times spiritually draining.

Pride in the fact that we know that physical strength leads to mental strength leads to spiritual strength leads to increased physical strength. It is a circle of self-feeding power and victory. Our triumphs are unknown and unsung — they are for us! They are our personal glories and we know that with each personal accomplishment in the realm of physical might we grow stronger as a human being, more apt to take on new challenges and overcome them with the same dedication and ferocity with which we attack the Iron.

A healthy, strong body is the only appropriate conveyance for a healthy, strong mind.

# XXIV.
# BE CONSISTENT

TRANSMISSION DATE: 03-19-15

We are all guilty of losing forward motion from time to time — of questioning our training methods just a little too much, or changing them around too often. Getting sidetracked by our day to day and missing more than a few days a week of our program of physical and spiritual domination.

"Off" days will happen- those days where you're just not fully "there" mentally, or when your body is feeling beat down, weak, or not as committed as your mind to the task at hand. On days like this, one has to remind themselves not to be too dis-heartened — the important thing is: you're there.

Every fucking day, your level of dedication is such that you push yourself to show up, knowing that just being there and doing the work is half the battle.

In a conversation with some comrades today, we imagined what our level of progress would be if we had all remained consistent in our weight training from the time when we started. It was a sobering thought- even if one could hypothetically add 10 pounds to each exercise a month, or thereabouts — with proper nutrition and training, the amount of weight being moved now, some 12 years of inconsistent training, nutrition, poor lifestyle choices, injuries and so on later… well, do the math.

It is very common to see folks be hard on themselves for these "off" days.

Just remember: you are building an empire here, not a tent village. It takes time. There will be days where more or less progress happens, or when it feels like you've hit a plateau for weeks at a time. Just show up. Be consistent. Track your progress by religiously keeping a journal of your training and nutrition each day. Keep working harder — and anytime anyone tries to draw you into some new fad, just keep in mind the fact that the bench, the deadlift, the squat, and the overhead press will always be the four pillars of strength. Doing them regularly at increasing weight/repetition will ALWAYS make you stronger.

# XXV.
# FEAR NOT LIVING

## By: Eoghan, WoV

TRANSMISSION DATE: 03-20-15

One day you are going to die. It is an inevitable fact. It might be today, tomorrow, six years or sixty from now. It might be lung cancer, a heart attack, a car accident, a bullet, or simply not waking up one morning. Death does not care if you are wealthy or poor, it does not discriminate.

The simple fact is that if there is no death, there is no life. The sunset and cherry blossom are so beautiful because they are fleeting. Life is no different.

In modern society, death is not spoken of openly. When it is spoken of, it is construed as a negative thing, as something to be beaten. "The leading cause of death is thus-and-such, so quit doing it." The leading cause of death is, in fact, life. Some of the choices we make might expedite that, but those are our choices. It's life. Death is natural, and it is a part of being alive.

> "The fear of death follows from the fear of life. A man who lives fully is prepared to die at any time." — Mark Twain

Those who are most afraid to die are those who procrastinate, they are those who have put off until tomorrow what they are fully capable of doing today. People often speak of a "bucket list," all the things that they plan on doing if they find out they have a terminal illness. The things they want to do when they know they are dying. Yet, they have missed the irony. You are dying from the moment you took your first breath. Every day you are healthy and virile and you just see it as a "normal day" is the day to check things off your bucket list. Right now is the only guaranteed time, so why waste it?

Every day, I wake up and I look in the mirror and honestly tell myself that this is my last day. I sing my own dirge, and I ready my mind and spirit for the end. Some people might say that it is morbid, but I face reality, and I am free because of it. Because I embrace death, instead of fear it, I am able to fully experience life without worry. The sunrise is beautiful because it is the last one I will ever see, the wind and the rain and the laughter of children and each deed I perform is mighty because those things might be the last I experience. There is life in every breath.

Do not be afraid of death, for death will one day come for us regardless of our fear. Be afraid of not living, because that ultimately falls upon our shoulders, and none other.

# XXVI.
## THE FEMALE OPERATIVE

### By: M. Rosa

TRANSMISSION DATE: 03-20-2015

*For our female operatives, we announce* Project She-Wolf. *Geared toward fitness and traditional female values for the physical y fit and radical y minded woman outside of time.*
— P.W.

You do not have to sacrifice your individuality for embracing your femininity. Personal power is gained from knowing yourself and maintaining integrity to your own values.

In a gym setting, this is obtained through logging goals and progress.

For women, the importance of logging has double significance. As your hormones fluctuate throughout each monthly cycle you absolutely need to know how this is going to affect you and your training program. These factors also depend on the type of training you're doing, i.e. endurance or strength training. If you start to feel a loss of stamina during certain parts of your cycle, you need to show up and be honest with yourself.

Log your mental state for a few months and compare. Does your stamina dip down during luteal phase? Are you craving more carbs during a certain phase? Does your emotional state affect the mental control you have to overcome a slack attitude and laziness? Learn these things about yourself and overcome those weaknesses. Don't forget to date your entries. This is especially important if you are a woman, due to the fact that you need to know if you are on a 24 day cycle, a 28 day cycle etc. You need to know what to expect and when.

After you have logged these things, do some research. There are a lot of factors that will help you immensely when it comes to planning your lifting schedule. In saying that, research is very important, but nothing is more important than knowing how your personal body chemistry works and how you will react during your training. This is why it is doubly important for women to understand and find a way to sync up with the natural flow of their body, not fight it. It doesn't have to be traumatic. If you do the work in your logging, you're less apt to feel upset when you gain 5 - 10 pounds of water weight and temporarily lose the cuts you've been working for. You can also mentally prepare for these substantial body changes if you know what to expect. Additionally, you can learn how to make small-scale changes that will lead you down the path of embracing and honoring yourself in and out of the gym.

As a final note to this opening transmission: Female operatives — please be aware of the outright attack on your personal power. The modern feminist movement is counter productive and demonizes a traditional woman's role by implying that it makes her inferior. Do not condone this this by acting like a "bro" in the gym. You are woman - act like one, in and out of the gym.

There is no need to walk like a man, talk like a man and embrace all that is "masculine."

Once you fail to recognize your very unique and important role as a woman in a family (and a society), a breakdown of the family (and society) results. The entirety of what you support cannot be strong if you are not strong as a woman. Do not support the disgusting ignorant trend that borders on androgynous behavior! You are not a non-person. You are not a part of the herd. You are bigger than that! You can celebrate your assets daily by honoring yourself, and strengthening yourself in the gym. Be an example for those around you who have lost their way. Change yourself first, and find yourself in a position of personal strength and power. This is the only way: Fight for what you believe in, train hard, eat clean and be strong.

# XXVII.
# WE ARE THE VILLANS

## TRANSMISSION DATE: 03-30-15

Just as the Wolf does not justify itself to its prey, Strength does not justify itself to Weakness. The choices that we make, the symbols we use, the terminology that we have chosen, we have done so consciously, with purpose.

Our purpose is unclear to those who cannot understand the thought process that would drive someone to use these words and signs of a bygone age to rekindle a primal flame, to use wording that has no soft edges, no mercy, no time to concern itself with fragile feelings or those that it might offend — our methods will show themselves as effective not through reasoning or argument, association with political ideas, empty posturing and so on, but through action.

Aleister Crowley poignantly said, in regards to the practice of occult methods, "Success is your only proof." These words ring true for us, as well.

No amount of talk or intellectualism can replace action and experience. Arguing your methods with those who will never grasp them is the height of worthless folly.

Time spent in useless dialogue with the uncomprehending masses of slave-minds could be better used sharpening your own mind, improving your body, your skill-sets, feeding your savage nature, strong in the knowledge that you answer to yourself alone, for there is no higher authority to a man that truly knows himself and is capable of being a true Anarch. This rulership over our base self, the relationship between Thrall mind and Tyrant mind is at the heart of Operation Werewolf, and those that understand this principle of self-dictatorship can grasp the use of our imagery in the way intended — those who cannot, will not.

Go forth in power, make of yourself a legend, unconcerned with the detractions and accusatory shrieking of the hollow ghosts that populate this world. Always remember that on the road of Heroes, there are many adversaries who will paint you as a Villain, and rightly so, because in an age of filth and depravity, insanity and weakness — we are the Villains.

# XXIX.
# YOU DON'T DESERVE
# A GODDAMN THING

TRANSMISSION DATE: 03-09-15

You don't deserve a goddamn thing. Whoever told you otherwise was wrong. Nothing in this life comes easy, or comes without a struggle. That struggle — that constant overcoming of self, of obstacle, of opponent— is where glory is won, and heroes are made. The difference between the strong and the weak is all in our approach to this struggle. Do we embrace it with gritted teeth and blood in our eyes, ready to fuck it or beat it into submission so that we become stronger in our next confrontation with adversity, or do we shy away from it, slinking into our holes like a whipped dog?

This existence is war, and we are poised to become legends or lickspittles, bronze statues or bitches. There is no time to falter or flail in the quicksand of modern niceties, or to fight your battles with the rules that they have laid out for you. Victory is the only option, the only thing worth focusing on — but this, too, is where the hard are separated from the herd. Our struggle, our war — is ongoing. It is neverending. There will never be a time of peace in our lives, because the battle is both internal and external, it is fought against the slave-self and the very real enemies who are arrayed against us in the physical realm. It is spiritual warfare as much as literal warfare.

Because of this, those who grow weary of conflict will capitulate to the brutal and endless strife, opting out with an excuse on their lips and the fire in their blood extinguished. Beaten down, they will retreat from the front lines and settle for a straw-death, their names unspoken even by their immediate offspring.

It is only the True, their hearts filled with the Smokeless Fire, who will go on to be renowned by future generations as heroes, although today's degenerates will label them the worst of villains and revile them. They will go on because they know they are owed nothing. They deserve nothing beyond what the strength of their Will, their Mind, their Spirit, and their Arm can take and hold.

Awaken into each dawn with war in your blood, fire in your heart, death in your eyes and words of overcoming and brotherhood on your lips.

Burn your opposition on the pyre of total devastation, and let its light shine brightly to beckon others to the funeral feast. Make pacts with the strong, and together, march forward into legend.

# XXIX.
# IRON MEN FOR AN IRON AGE

TRANSMISSION DATE: 03-16-15

In the text *Bhagavata Purana*, there is a list of predictions regarding the current Iron Age in which we live, the so-called Kali Yuga. It is said that morality, physical strength, duration of life expectancy will all diminish to a point of extreme lowness. We are told that wealth alone will determine a man's social standing, as well as his treatment by the justice system. Men and women will only judge each other by sexual attraction, and that the desire for food, sex and money will be the only real drive remaining. All spiritual truths will become corrupted, and politicians and merchants will consume the citizenship of Empire.

We can see these predictions as obvious truths in our current world — modernity is a sea of filth and depravity, neatly packaged and sold as the ideal way of life, an illusion spun by merchant and media to draw all citizens under its seductive spell. The first step toward strength is to recognize this falsehood for what it is: a diseased prostitute, with her legs spread on the altar of consumption and distraction- veiled and perfumed to fool the unwitting, but rotten with open sores underneath. We must look to something more, some higher standard, knowing that our destiny is not to live as a slave of money, media, mass-production and monoculture.

What then, in this age of falsity and weakness, makes a man truly strong? How can he set out to become what we all must, a devotee of Kalki, the Destroyer of Filthiness, swords drawn and ready to make a purifying war against the lie of Progress?

Firstly, he must be focused and vital, eliminating as much useless distraction from his life as possible. He must know that the greatest weapon of the lords of Empire is this distraction from Purpose, and be aware of its wide-flung net. Honesty with the self is the best way forward through this morass.

What is truly necessary in our lives and serves the greater narrative of our living mythology? What actions will forward our legend, serve to make us stronger, call out to others seeking this path — and what actions are a waste of our precious time? What saps our vitality, removes our drive, crumbles our motivation? A simple and honest self-critique of the ways we spend our time throughout the day will often show us a sobering reality. Recognizing that our addictions are not always to drink or drug, but to social media, iPhones, Netflix, and so on is the first step to eliminating their influence on our lives.

When the addiction is eliminated, the mental fog of too much distraction, technology, useless information, begins to clear and opens the way forward.

Once we have cleared much of the debris from our daily lives, what should we fill it with? What does the strong man do with his time to develop his higher self, to make himself into the warrior, the tribal leader, the wolf-masked transcendent berserker?

He trains his physical form and tests that form through competition — he knows that to be whole and healthy is the foundation of a solid character, and he achieves this through a disciplined regimen of strength and martial training.

A powerful man is capable of the defense of himself and those close to him, not reliant on the corrupt servants of Empire to protect his life and limb, and in order to do so, he must be a specimen of physical might and terrible in combat.

Simply put, an able-bodied man who is not physically imposing and ready to perform violence in a skilled fashion is not a real man at all.

He trains his mental faculties through the study of the world around him with a critical and uncompromising gaze, knowing that his ascension cannot remain merely physical. He seeks out direct experience with an adventurous heart, not content to learn from others, hungry for life — cracking the longbones of this existence and sucking out the marrow. His wisdom grows from this relentless experiencing of life, and he becomes one who others seek out for advice and guidance, a credit to his tribe through the two pillars of Being and Doing.

His spirit is strengthened through the recognition of his place as the spearhead of his ancestral line, the forefront of a waterfall of blood that has come before him, and honors that awful responsibility by living his life in a worthy fashion. He learns the history, cultures and ritual of his people and keeps that fire burning — in this fashion, he denies the horrifying de-humanizing monster of homogenous monoculture, keeping his identity and the identity of his people strong in the face of the hollowness and emptiness of consumerism.

He seeks out others who are or are becoming strong, and surrounds himself with people who challenge him, who recognize similar values and opens himself to confrontation from them. Without a peer group of powerful individuals, the lone wolf atrophies— he is not pressured to higher levels of existence, or held accountable to his words and deeds on a daily basis.

Strength loves strength, where weakness ridicules it. The man who remains among the weak forever will eventually become like them through association.

His tribe seeks out other tribes, looking to forge alliances with other powerful clans, men with blood staining their banners, outlaws in this age of feebleness and degeneracy. They create bonds spoken out under the stars, fires burning in their hearts as they cast their gaze toward the cities and prisons of the rotting carcass of Empire, and their strength becomes freedom.

The way forward from here is not yet clear, but it can never become so until we who would change and reforge this world can change and reforge ourselves into men that can create new legends. We must first destroy that

Great Enemy within before we can hope to survive against any enemy without — our weakness must be sacrificed on that blood red altar of Self-Transformation until the gods walk among men once again. Those gods will bear our names, our grim visages, and we will create this world anew from the ashes of the old one. 92/Iron & Blood!

# XXX.
# SYMBOL AND STRENGTH

TRANSMISSION DATE: 06-03-15

*The Winnowing*: The hollowness of modernity has shown itself to you, the operative, and you have chosen to strive for something more. The comfort in the mundane, in society's established forms are not for us. The Iron Age calls for Iron and the fighting of fire with fire. The stagnation and stasis of order can only be overcome with the Chaotic Anabolism. Nothing stops creating, the ceiling has been met and the Illusion of Progress fools Order into thinking that "That is enough..." With your eyes you've seen Order's negation of the primal and witnessed the creeping effeminacy and degeneracy of modernity and know that it is false.

*The Wolfhook*: The men that came before us believed in the power of symbolism. In antiquity the Folk knew our symbol to possess magical powers. They used it on their homes and on boundary markers to ward off predators and outsiders. Today the magic of the Wolfhook that adorns the Operative functions similarly, as a ward against decay and the catabolism of Order. Under this sign, the walls of True Will are bolstered and the Operative can then build.

*The Lighthouse*: The Operative salutes with the dominant hand, thumb, first and second finger outstretched with 3rd and 4th fingers clenched inward. A living ALGIZ. A symbol to always keep striving, a defiant pledge of the vitality of the ascendant. "Per Aspera Ad Astra".... "through hardship to the stars."

***Iron & Blood (the Lunar 92)***: Our watchwords are "Iron & Blood", symbolized by the 92 that falls under the auspices of the Moon, governance of the untamed Chaos of the tides and harbinger of lycanthropic transformation. Iron is the core of the Gods, the smell and taste of blood is of the smell and taste of the Gods, Gods who call us to shape ourselves in their image.

# XXXI.
# DIVISION

TRANSMISSION DATE: 06-16-15

As Werewolf Operatives across nations come together to form Divisions, and solitary practitioners fly the death-wolf standard to show their affiliation, the next step is considered: How will your Division function? What will it look like in practice, in form, in tribal marking?

After assembling at least 3 operatives and submitting the Division name and locale for approval, what comes next for the Division leader and the other operatives forming this new unit?

The answers to these questions vary entirely on the Division, but are important ones for the fledgling unit to decide upon. How tight the structure of a group is from the beginning will largely determine its function later on down the road — an organization that begins in a loose and more organic form will most likely remain that way, as it is difficult to add rigidity to a structure after its inception. A Division that begins in a more ordered and structured fashion will obviously have a different look and feel, and because of this, will find itself fulfilling a different function than others.

Although all Operatives bear the Totenwolf, there are myriad ways a Division can mark itself to promote unit pride and a sense of tribalism within. Specific colors used, patches, paint, or by-words in line with the chosen Division name; specialty within the larger network of operatives by skillset — for example a Division led by someone who instructs Muay Thai is likely to have a heavier focus on training for conditioning and hand-to-hand than one led by a powerlifter. In this way, an Operative in the future will have choices available to him when he considers what Division appeals to him most based on its form and function, and can look to undergo the tests and trials required by that unit in order to become a member.

This leads us to our next question: What will Divisions require of new members, or veteran Operatives who are applying to join their Division? Will there be a boot camp of sorts, or a "prospecting/probationary" period? Will it be open to any and all to join? Are there specific requirements for this Division that makes it different from others, or more specialized? These issues need to be addressed upon the formation of a new Division and clearly understood by its members before events are put on and things begin to take shape.

Obviously, the emphasis in Operation Werewolf is face-to-face meetings, and the development of Divisions that meet regularly, made up of individuals who want to push and be pushed to higher standards of physical, mental and spiritual performance. Because of this, it is important that Divisions begin holding regularly scheduled events, both on a private and open level. What this looks like, again, will be up to the Division. Private events can be monthly or weekly, but should not be less frequent than every other month at the very least, whether this is a meet-up at a gym, home location, training field, whatever. The activities should cover the physical, mental and spiritual spectrum, with all operatives coming away recharged and better for it.

An example of this would be the operatives meeting at a local gym or the garage gym of a member to lift weights and box or grapple, followed by a meal and group discussion regarding Divisional business. From there, a talk on what the operatives are doing to push themselves mentally — what books are being read, etc. This could be followed by a symbel, a ritual tradition that is incredibly bonding and strengthening. Those with a deeper interest in ritual or spiritual traditions can begin to develop these organically with the Division-down the road, each Division may have its own highly developed and extremely unique mythos around which these rituals are based.

The way forward is the Division — strong individuals are needed to form these Divisions: hard-chargers with a gut full of fire and a firm grasp on the tenets of Operation Werewolf. Leaders of men, illuminated barbarians prepared to undergo the Change — that lycanthropic shift from Man to Wolf symbolized by our Wolf-rune.

These men are berserkers charging towards Truth, gnashing their teeth against the falsehood and weakness of the Kali Yuga, not content to weep and give in to the beast of modernity — but to savagely charge it, leap upon its spear-wounded back and ride it into the ground! In order to re-establish value in this world, we must give worth and life back to those principles which promote strength and fierce joy: physical power, mental sharpness, spiritual depth, brotherhood and sisterhood, tribe, ferocity and laughter at this wondrous thing called Life that pumps through our healthy veins.

Adventure and experience create powerful humans. Faced alone, they are an enjoyable challenge. Faced with brothers, they are a true joy for the man who knows the invincibility which tribe can bring. 92!

# XXXII.
# ACHIEVING CONSONANCE

## The Principles of Self-Creation, Part One

TRANSMISSION DATE: 06-23-15

The sun beat down on me mercilessly- for 9 hours and counting I had been roaring across the Colorado landscape on a chopped Victory motorcycle. My battle jacket was snapping in the wind, the white wolf-head backpatch signifying my tribal affiliation flying proud, if the bold "WOLVES" ink across my throat wasn't indicator enough.

Easing off the throttle, I turned into the gravel strewn parking lot of a small convenience store, my throat dry as a bone — no room for niceties like saddle-bags and supplies on this death machine. As I dismounted, knocking some of the dust off my black Levi's, and pulling down the bandana from my face, I took a second to admire the bike I'd been on all day. It looked just like I wanted it to- flat black, rugged as hell, pipe-wrapped and nasty, no signals or instrument array; a big fucking V-twin with tires and a saddle seat and not much else.

Walking toward the gas station, I caught a glimpse of myself in the big window out front, and was struck with a similar feeling I'd just had as I looked at the motorcycle. I was looking at the product of 30 years of effort, experience, artistry and hard work; a lot of mistakes that had to be buffed out and repaired. More than a few collisions on the way, a network of scars from my face on down to my busted up, tattooed knuckles, but still more than just "functional."

As the idea took root, I began considering other aspects and areas of my life, and thinking about their connection to one another, long after I finished the cold drink and mounted back up on that horse for the last stretch of highway back to Cheyenne. It led me to a few realizations, and I decided to put them down in writing for those who might be able to use them:

Consonance in your life is everything. If you are living in a fashion that many of your endeavors either do not complement one another, or worse, contradict each other, you are treading water in random directions and will never reach the shore. Think long and hard about what it is you want, and where you are attempting to go, and make your actions congruent with that goal. Think of your life as a single canvas, one that you are putting a lifetime's work of art on- chaos can be beautiful, but even within chaos, patterns begin to emerge. Focus on those patterns, the strong points, or the theme of the piece, and reinforce it — push it along those pathways with encouragement by feeding the strengths that you wish to see grow. You cannot serve more than one master. Life may not be "short," as in fact, it is the longest endeavor we will ever undertake, but it certainly is not there for the wasting. Embrace it fully, but know that you cannot attain greatness while constantly distracted. Once you have discovered your Great Work (more on this discovery process in the next installment), any action that does not take you toward this is a betrayal of Self. Be conscious in all your actions and words-does this action strengthen or catalyze you on the road to becoming what and who you want to be? If not, it can be done without. This kind of thinking lends meaning to seemingly mundane action — even the simple process of eating becomes a deeper idea entirely — as we realize that we are fueling the body in order to undertake and live out our chosen destiny, will we make better choices in what we put into our body, the physical conveyance of the Holy Fire? This goes for all habits that we see as unproductive or actions that "lessen" us, or dampen our flame. Choices create habit. Neuroscience has shown us that repetitive thought strengthens pathways in our brain, for good or ill, and that we have control over this process based around how we think and what types of thinking we choose to reinforce. A strong, positive and confident mindset actually makes us stronger, more positive, more confident, because we have begun to make it the "default" setting for our brain. Similarly, the actions that we take in our life set the stage for more of the same. If we deal with the world around us from a position of strength and confidence, we will begin to do this habitually. If we choose to fight instead of flee, we are more likely to fight each time, to stand our ground — if instead, we seek to escape conflict, we program that into ourselves, and it becomes a harder mode to break with each action that reinforces it as "who we are." This is why it is even more important to live with consonance — the more we undertake those actions and think with those mindsets that propel us along our chosen path, the stronger those impulses will be, the more powerful we will be when we meet obstacle and opponent on that road. We are not enslaved to our past. Although in the previous paragraph, we discussed the idea of self-programming, it is not permanent. It must be reinforced — it can also be broken. Every bad habit, from smoking cigarettes to acting with cowardice can be destroyed, re-programmed, until the hero we've become is nothing like the human we allowed ourselves to be.

It is easy to be weak, lazy, undirected. Because of this, we must work hard to create those pathways, those circuits of Action, scoring them into the very surface of our Being, so that the blood runs easier and easier into their channels. After mis-steps and mistakes, trial and error, I have begun to achieve that consonance and I can FEEL it — obstacles crumbling, opponents rising in great number, only to be conquered. The more powerful we become, often, the more detractors we have — flies buzzing around us in the marketplace. Those who must crawl will always despise those with wings, but we must constantly Keep Rising, Ever Higher, Ever Onward. 92!

# XXXIII.
# SAGA BUILDING

## The Principles of Self-Creation, Part Two

TRANSMISSION DATE: 08-20-2015

"But not all men seek rest and peace- some are born with the spirit of the storm in their blood." — Robert E. Howard

The men who came before us created legends. Songs and sagas were written about their exploits, and some of their names have survived thousands of years to still be spoken by the tongues of those unworthy to even pronounce them. When we think of Achilles, Egil Skalagrimsson, Arminius — we understand them as archetypes; their names have transcended simple story and have taken on weight and meaning as symbols of might and power. They have become what I call "living runes," flesh and blood sigils that course with the power of a life lived for strength.

These individuals have given us templates to follow — emulatable modes of being that embrace the bride named Hardship, worship at the altar called Ordeal and die for the immortality we know as Glory. Their stories must make us take a hard look at the stories we are living, and ask a few questions of ourselves:

*Would our lives be a story worth telling?*

*What makes a life worth remembering, or simpler yet, worth living at all?*

*What is the contrast between their lives and ours?*

*What can be done to reawaken the spirit of adventure and heroism?*

To answer these we must firstly look at our habits, the everyday deeds that take up the greater portion of our lives. We are given this one life to live, to accomplish greatness. How are we spending it? Are we using the majority of our waking hours working a mundane job that gives us no value, provides us with no challenge, no adventure, and eats up time that we could be spending scaling the mountains of Experience and Trial? What sort of care are we taking of our bodies? Do we let the sand run from our finite glass while carousing and drinking ourselves blind as a shortcut to enjoyment? Are those hundreds of hours (the ones that can be remembered) and dollars that are expended in the bar creating happiness, or fulfilling a greater sense of purpose?

In order to be a story worth telling, your life must be made up of trial and ordeal. In order for this to happen, you must break out of your comfort zone and place yourself into situations that are unknown and difficult, and conquer them.

A life spent in mindless labor, trivial pursuits, and the fulfillment of base desires is not only boring, plain and normal- it is not one that is even worth living. By living this way, you are one of billions of people on this planet living essentially the exact same life, with only minor discrepancies between the two. You are only serving as the tiniest, most insignificant piece in a machine larger than your imagining, and when your light goes out, you are infinitely replaceable and no one will notice your passing.

Would you not prefer, if this life is all we have, to cast off the shackles of normalcy, to embrace adventure, and to create a saga from your life, and the lives of those who might join you, and use your time on this earth to live such a tale of wonder that your name is remembered for a thousand years? To achieve this, we have to stop thinking of life as a system in which we must work, rent, pay, eat, marry, raise, die — or, as I said in the original Operation Werewolf transmission, we have to break the cycle of masticate, defecate, procreate, disintegrate. We must begin to perceive life as the game that it is, a game in which it is always our turn.

Choosing a life of adventure is not escapism — it is creationism. It is deciding that you will not be held down by rules that you did not agree to, and that you gave no consent to this way of life that has been put forth as "the norm", and that you will simply do better.

The next steps are up to you, but here are some suggestions:

Train your mind and body. Be healthy and strong, and ready for anything.

Take up a martial art, or weightlifting, or better yet, both. If unsure of where to begin, feel free to send me a message at grimnir1984@gmail.com and I will get you started with a plan of nutrition and fitness that will increase the value of your life immensely, and allow you to take further steps on the road toward being exceptional instead of normal.

Every week, pick three things that you will accomplish that are outside your comfort zone. Whether this is running 3 miles (or even three blocks —know yourself well enough to know your limitations— this is the best way to destroy your limitations!), climbing a mountain, or a public speaking engagement, there is no way to become a legend if you remain within your comfort zone! Challenge yourself. Keep going forward until the only way to challenge yourself is with acts of total heroism.

Compete. Find things you enjoy doing, and become competitive. Enter a grappling contest, or submit your artwork or writing to a publication or contest. Go run a 5k. Whatever it is you like, test it against others in your field, and keep expanding "your field."

Always look to surround yourself with people who challenge you. Life is too fucking short to be around mediocre people who are doing nothing with themselves. Choose your friends wisely — it's been said that you are the average of the five people you spend the most time with. Think about this when you are out with your "crew" and decide whether you want to be the average of them or not. Good friends will push you to become more than you are. Bad friends will try to get you to remain at their level.

Whatever you decide to do, know that this world is still full of wildness, of savagery, of wonder and adventure. It will not present itself to you while you are sitting on your couch watching Netflix. Get up, right now, and go do something incredible. 92!

# XCII.
# TRANSMISSION 92

TRANSMISSION DATE: 06-30-15

Mixing together equal parts fight club, strength regimen, motorcycle club and esoteric order, Operation Werewolf is more than the sum of its parts. It is not an organization, but an organism- living and breathing by its tenets and watchwords, "Iron and Blood."

It is an affiliation of strength — Wolves among men who recognize one another by the three fingered salute and by the black flag that is their shirt, tank top or battle jacket that reads "Operation Werewolf." These men and women have chosen to gather under this banner because it calls out to their primal natures, that fiery blood that sets them apart from the hopeless grey masses that wander this rock devoid of purpose or joy.

Operatives can be found in countries across the world, dripping sweat on the floor of their spartan-style garage weight room, leaving blood on the dirt in the backyard boxing ring, or bringing their feral competitive style to powerlifting meets, MMA events, bars, back alleys and the savage streets of crumbling cities. They are not products of their environment — instead they change the landscape and environment around them, forgers of destiny, architects of their own becoming. They make the flesh strong, knowing that it is the only fit conveyance for a strong mind and an iron will — theirs is a mindset that accepts no weakness.

Some are solitary practitioners, performing the rituals of life and death amongst the ruins of modern civilization, lone wolves howling songs of destruction and new growth in the woods that encroach on the edges of the rotting Empire, waiting for the fall. Others have made it their mission to seek each other out, forming militaristic divisions, chapters led by their strongest member, creating a war-band that seeks to carve its own myth, to create its own saga of power and might- men and women challenging each other to strive ever higher.

It is not a political statement, but a bloody fist shaken in the face of all institutions of control — a furious bite to the hands that seek to leash or enslave. It is not right or left, but free of these shackles of modern dualistic thinking — it operates under the assumption that the Kings of this world have become so through the forked tongue of finance and fear, and it rejects their offerings. The warriors who make up Operation Werewolf know that the true heroes are those who are self-made, physically and mentally strong, free thinkers and free doers who are both untamed and unrepentant.

Operation Werewolf is a lifestyle, one of constant self-overcoming and hardship. You operatives know that today's effort is tomorrow's reward, and that one must always strive to outdo themselves — each day must be lived as though it is Ragnarok, each hour the last one of our lives.

So make of your bodies a temple, of your will a weapon, of your mind a smokeless fire that reduces this world's lies into ashes. Iron and Blood!

# XXXV.
# ADVENTURE

TRANSMISSION DATE: 07-13-15

About two years ago, I made the conscious decision that I was done with the nine to five lifestyle. I'd had enough of working all week and winding up with nothing to show for it after my bills were paid, and realized that no matter how much I made (or didn't make) in a week, I was usually still struggling financially, the only difference being, on weeks I worked less, I got more done.

Somehow, on those tight weeks, I would always find some kind of side work or hustle to make it by, getting the amounts needed for basic survival and paying the rent, often times booking some last minute gigs to play music for my dinner (literally), or picking up a bouncing shift at a local bar.

I started to think: why can't I just do this every week? Be my own boss, or at the very least, choose the work I wanted to do as necessary for survival instead of having my entire existence defined by a job that I didn't particularly care for in the first place. If I limited my bills to things that I actually needed, and found ways to bring in extra for the little luxuries, could I walk away from the 40 hour a week grind that seems to dominate the way we think about labor in this day and age? I quit my job and began making about ninety percent of my income on music and merch, bouncing a few times a week, and doing the occasional odd job.

I discovered that I had an amazing amount of free time available, and that the amount of currency that came to me actually reflected how hard I worked and how much time I put in to my own endeavors, rather than a set rate by a corporate employer. I found a great deal of satisfaction in that, and that each dollar made was made by me, for me — nothing went up the chain to some overlord. It was a turning point for me, and I have not worked a "normal" job since.

The point of all this is that our lives are our art. How can we work on a masterpiece if all our time is taken up doing work to make someone else rich? How will we have the time or inclination for adventure when we are exhausted from breaking our backs for another's wealth? Our sole endeavor should be to create lives in which we see real value, and that fulfill us in a deep and satisfying way, lives of glorious experience and inspiring action. As I had it put to me once, if you were a character in a movie, would you be the main character or a supporting role? We need to create something of ourselves that is larger than life, vibrant, full of savage joy at the wide range of awesome deeds there are to sample in our time here, and that cannot be done by living a "normal" life.

What I would recommend is for anyone unsatisfied with themselves, their situation, their current life: sit down and write down a list with two columns. In the one column, write down every characteristic about yourself that you see as a strength or an asset, such as special skills you have, or characteristics that are unique. In the other column, being brutally honest, write down everything you see as a weakness, or would like to change about yourself. Write out below this a paragraph or so that outlines how you would like to be as a person, how you would like to be perceived by others. Be creative and honest here as well — like creating a character for a novel, you can write anything you like here; think big, and don't limit yourself with doubt or what you think is "realistic." Just write it.

Your new goal, each day, is to consciously work toward finding ways to apply those strengths to ideas that can make you more financially independent. Are you an artist or graphic designer? Start doing commissioned work on the side. Not good enough at it? Improve. Are you a musician? Learn to busk, or book some gigs and learn to haggle for a good guarantee or sell more merchandise. Are you physically imposing? Take some extra work as a doorman, or work toward a personal trainer's license. Writer? There are numerous paying jobs for writers on the internet if one applies themselves to searching them out. Skilled in a trade? Advertise your services on craigslist or the local paper. You'd be surprised how many people still find help this way.

As for the second column, your job is to select one of those weaknesses EVERY FUCKING DAY and force yourself into a situation that makes you confront that weakness and allows the opportunity to reset your neural pathways of behavioral patterns in order to reduce that weakness. Cowardly? Start training at an MMA gym and look to compete in local amateur fighting events. Shy? Assign yourself the task of talking to strangers and improving your conversational abilities, even if it is at first painfully difficult to do so. Overweight? Choose and adhere to a diet and exercise regimen, as if your life depends on it- because it does.

After doing this method for a few months, you will begin to form yourself into the paragraph you have written, and every day you wake up, you will affirm yourself as that person you wanted to become, not with empty words or prayers, but through laborious action and deed filled with intention and will.

As you become more stable and independent, your avenues of adventure will open up — when you do not have to report in to a life of drudgery each morning, many doors unlock. Experiences can be chased after on a whim, as should be the case with everyone — life should be your oyster, not your prison. Visit new cities, and meet interesting people — in some cases, fight those people! Come out of your shell and speak with force and power about your passions, and inspire others to higher deed and lives of mighty expression.

Life, at its core, is only as meaningful as we choose to make it. It can be filled with excitement, adventure, varied experience, or it can be a drab, dull thing of repetition and shallowness. We have only to look at it as a great tree filled with many fruits, and know that it is all ours for the tasting. Go forth, and conquer! 92.

# XXXVI.
# PRINCIPLES OF VIOLENCE

*An Interview With Johnny Pain*

TRANSMISSION DATE: 07-17-15

My first exposure to Johnny Pain was, like many others, his image plastered on cut scenes of the often-times-ridiculous show "Gangland," which was doing a piece on a group he had been affiliated with several years ago — the hardcore scene crew F.S.U. (an acronym for either Friends Stand United or Fuck Shit Up, depending on who you ask).

After this, the next time I saw his tattooed mug was on the cover of the e-book "The Greyskull Lifting Program," which I had sought out through interest in a basic, no-bullshit, effective method of strength building. I used the GSLP in various incarnations for most of a year and saw good gains with it, and some of the stuff included in that book and a few others I got my hands on provoked some curiosity in me about the man himself.

Some cursory Google searches on Johnny Pain turns up a few facts that I related to pretty well: one, that he has a tendency to shake shit up wherever he goes, blazing a trail where he wants it to go rather than being content to follow in others footsteps, and two, that people either seem to love him or utterly despise him. I figured that I wasn't going to be able to make much of a determination one way or the other without a face to face meeting, and I had seen that he was putting on a seminar/workshop called "Principles of Personal Defense" at the one and only Greyskull Barbell Club on the outskirts of one of America's grimiest cities, Philadelphia, PA.

I am a spur of the moment kinda guy, and I figured I'd do this for the same reason I do most things- the sheer experience of it (or, as John would say, and has tatted on his face, "For the story"). A weekend hanging out with a guy feared throughout the Philly underworld (just ask around about him — from one percenter outlaw bikers to guys in the metal scene there, everyone had a story about him it seemed like) sounded like just my kind of weekend, and I was genuinely interested in what a course designed to prepare the participant for experiences with "asocial violence" might look like.

My woman and I threw a backpack in the car and made the six and a half hour drive up to Philly, saw our first coke deal within ten minutes of getting out of the car at a local bar (standard sights of the city), crashed at a friend's, and headed for Greyskull Barbell Club on Saturday morning ready to get our hands dirty.

The first thing that greeted us upon walking in to the place in all its gritty glory were the massive wall hangings reading "VILLAIN," another parallel between JP and my branding, for those familiar with one of the Operation Werewolf slogans. The gym itself is like something out of Rocky's wet dreams, a concrete floored warehouse, with one side dominated by old-school strength training gear, barbells, a few power racks and a lat pulldown machine so old it looked like the very one that Jesus might have used to build up his hanging muscles. The other half of the place was matted out and simple, ready for the weekend's event.

We made our introductions to the other handful of people there for the workshop, including Blake, Johnny's right hand man for this event, a fireplug of a Canadian who rattled off nonstop "facts" about his homeland all weekend that became both less believable and more depraved as the day wore on. I won't go into the definition of a "Canadian handshake" or the traditional holiday's practices that range from murderous to pornographic, but I will be visiting our northern neighbors in the hope that at least some of them are true.

Johnny arrived and introduced himself in his trademark relaxed, quiet tone and took a few minutes to talk with everyone before we sat down to business and the work began in earnest. What struck me immediately was his easygoing manner, and as the day went on, it displayed itself in a coaching style that kept all participants relaxed but focused, receptive to information conveyed in a humorous, often self-deprecating style, and even in correction made people feel at ease and confident.

Day one involved a lot of basics, going over everything from the main goal of an asocially violent situation (crippling, rendering unconscious, or killing all opposition in the most effective and rapid fashion), to developing a "vocabulary" of targets on the human body, each with their own specific spinal reflex that can be exploited in order to cause the greatest injury. Each topic was explained in depth, and drilled over and over to ensure the participants were familiar with each term and technique. From superior cervical ganglion to metatarsals, we were given informative and brutal methods to put to use in the drills, which consisted of one on one situational and free fighting using what had just been learned.

Saturday was a long one, and by the end of it, everyone was ready for a break. I had a gig in the city that evening, and couldn't join the rest of the crew, having to hear about the evening's degeneracy second hand the next morning as a (slightly hung over) cast of characters assembled to start the second day's training. Sunday was even more intensive than the day prior, as we began with free fighting drills to warm-up. All students were amazingly fluid even after a single grueling day of instruction, and then more info was brought into the mix. Multiple attackers, knife and gun strategies, ground fighting, disarming, limb breaks and more were thrown in, and the day became a blur of strikes, throws, grunts of spinal reflex reactions, and sweat. All questions were deftly answered and responses demonstrated in effective fashion.

Johnny was ever-present, walking through the room, watching first one trainee and speaking words of either correction or encouragement, then moving to the next, sometimes slowing down the combat to offer knowledge, or moving the participants to greater intensity.

At the end of Sunday's testing (all received a passing grade, I am pleased to say), we were exhausted but well informed. The day continued with dinner and drinks at JP's favorite local watering hole, and the night went on until the next morning...I'll spare folks the details of the mayhem that ensued, but suffice it to say, Greyskull Barbell Club knows how to party with the best of them.

All in all, The Principles of Personal Defense weekend seminar was extremely informative and highly recommended for those people who question their ability (or would like to increase their skill level) at dealing with an asocially violent situation. This is not about handling a fist fight at the local pub- it is designed for situations of extreme violence and hostility, in which throwing a triangle choke on an attacker is going to get you shot. There is a time and a place for jiu jitsu and boxing — a home invasion by multiple armed assailants is not it, a point driven home by the shooting of a prominent Brazilian jiu jitsu practitioner this month when he tried to apply a choke hold to an armed man. He was shot in the head for his trouble.

Those who are interested in Greyskull Academy Of Combat Sciences can go to strengthvillain.com to check out Johnny's ebooks (notably Principles of Violence), and to stay abreast of future seminars and workshops open to the public. To close this article, here is a Q and A session between me and the man himself. Ladies and gents, Johnny Pain:

*1) For those not familiar, why don't you tell us a bit about who you are, and how you cut your teeth on coaching everything from strength training, combatives, personal effectiveness and so on?*

[JP] Wow, well that's been a hell of a journey.

A few friends of mine joke that I must have come out of the womb teaching somebody something (or at least attempting to), and another good friend regularly states that, "the thing about JP is that he'll read a book on open heart surgery and then try his hand at it tomorrow".

I've been a voracious reader since I learned the all-valuable skill, and to date still read at least two books per week. When I get into something I have to know all I can learn about it, and test and challenge any "accepted truths" that exist in the subject matter.

I built an outdoor gym in my backyard years ago, after I returned home from Afghanistan, and in short order I had people wanting to train with me. From there, my quest for more knowledge resulted in my meeting the manager of a local posh, personal training gym while at a seminar in Minnesota. He invited me to check the place out, offered me a job as a "boot camp" instructor (it was a hell of a lot of fun having rich people do pushups in the mud and rain), and I quickly developed a strong client base in one-on-one personal training, which I never really intended to pursue.

From there it's a blur of affiliating with various major brands by way of their recruiting me, growing my personal base, and eventually parting ways with the organizations due to ideological or other types of differences that arose.

When I started answering nutrition questions on a popular training forum as the "diet guy", I became bombarded with requests for personal consultations via phone or Skype. I ran a solid business doing exactly that for a while (though my fees were ridiculously low compared to what they are today).

When I left that forum and organization, I started my own site and forum, and continued to consult and coach in a similar manner. It was around this time that I noticed some trends in the concerns that clients had, and began authoring books to address these issues for the masses.

Another offshoot of these calls however, was the more "personal" nature of the coaching. Guys (and girls) would ask me questions that had nothing to do with their training or diet, and more about their personal lives. Being a life-long student of personal development, NLP, Ericksonian hypnosis, and just having amassed a substantial amount of life experience, I was able to help a lot of these individuals, who then sung my praises to others.

A famous gossip columnist, who is a personal friend, dubbed me "the tattooed Tony Robbins". Beginning to offer and promote my services as a "Success Coach" was a bizarre, but smooth transition from there, and my practice is constantly growing.

These days I help a lot of "normal" guys break their mold and start a business, or just become more of a persuasive and dominant force in their environment. My video "What is Freedom" highlights this in more detail.

(https://www.youtube.com/watch?v=i_ULzG9TuRU)

As for the G/ACS, the path was a similar one: I was a combatives instructor while in the military, studied martial arts (from any source I could get my hands on) since I was a kid, and again challenged anything and everything that I thought wasn't useful.

I got linked up with a decent company that does a ton of high-dollar contract training with individuals and organizations all over the world, managed to piss a few people off internally, and walked away from a guaranteed high six-figure income with them to blaze my own trail.

I've since, of course, continued to evolve the information and curriculum, and have sought to teach the most effective, and simple to learn, scientific principles necessary for the individual or team to emerge victorious when it really counts, in an asocial situation.

I can honestly say that both my combat experience, and my propensity for "running with the wrong crowds" for many years enabled me to receive much insight that I believe a lot of the "armchair commando" types just flat out do not have.

Like I said, it's been a journey, and is an ongoing one. I work daily to develop and grow my own businesses, as well as assist clients with theirs, all while being a father to three kids, and an active asset to my community with organizations such as the VFW.

*2) What can someone expect to get out of your seminars and workshops, especially in regard to what you may have coming up that is open to the public?*

[JP] I believe in violating expectations with my events, in a positive way. I want every attendee to walk away with much more than they expected upon signing up.

The subject matter obviously differs depending on the event; personal development, strength training, entrepreneurship, or "combatives" for lack of a better term, but the constant is making sure that each attendee receives maximum value, and leaves with all of their questions asked.

I've also developed a bit of a reputation for....um.... hosting, I guess you could call it. Our "after event" get togethers are always epic, and attendees routinely say that they gained, learned, or valued as much if not more from the nights of the events as they did from the days of instruction.

As for an event schedule, that is always up in the air. Most of my events are created based on demand, and I do contract events on the road as well.

Basically if enough people want it, I launch a public event, and if someone contacts me to come to them with a check in their hand, I get something with them in the schedule.

Live events are, and have always been, my favorite aspect of my business.

*3) What are your plans for Greyskull Barbell/Academy of Combat Sciences in the future, and what can we expect to see from Johnny Pain this year?*

[JP] Again, this is a bit open at this point. Though I believe in, teach, and practice long term planning, I've found that, in my adult life, I've never accurately predicted where I would be a year from now. At this date I have two contract events coming up, one for a foreign military group, and one for a foreign law enforcement and corrections group. I'd like to see another public event in 2015, and will certainly try to get one setup if the schedule permits.

Otherwise, I'm working on a free product release that will open a lot of eyes to the "fallacies" that exist in the "self-defense" world, and will more than likely be following that up with a product that is dense with instruction. A more "advanced" series is incredibly easy to sell, but I prefer to know with conviction that the person has a solid grasp of the fundamentals before getting more advanced. This was one of the major conflicts I had with the organization that previously wanted me on board as an instructor, as they would pack classes with 30+ people at $1,000 or more per head, teach them a bunch of "lethal" shit, and still send more than half of them out of there ready to get their asses handed to them if they were in a real conflict that night.

I guess you can say that integrity has prevented me from making a lot more money from the GACS than I have, but ultimately it is what grows the brand.

*4) Final words, thoughts, rants or general degeneracy?*

[JP] Ahh... Fuck, Boobs, Tits, I suppose. I like all of those words.

As for degeneracy, I imagine that anyone wishing to see where I stand in that regard should hang out with Paul and I at some point. I mean, I am a professional after all.

# XXXVII.
# KEEPING THE FAITH

## TRANSMISSION DATE: 07-26-15

At times in our life, the biggest struggle we face is not an external one, but internal chaos: self-doubt, uncertainty, a lack of motivation or drive, or succumbing to despair after experiencing particularly crushing events.

When dealing with these negative feelings, it is easy to become rudderless — a ship adrift on the endless sea, with no guiding force or destination in sight. It can be very difficult to stay focused on our goals, and is impossible to create or sustain anything of greatness while we are under this sort of malaise. Often, individuals are permanently rendered useless by these great spells of blackness, allowing themselves to slip off into a place of total surrender, apathy, or depression, until they perceive it as too late to recover, and they accept their fate as a hungry ghost, gnashing their teeth in outer darkness.

We must not allow this to happen to ourselves — no matter the situation, no matter how grim the horizon, or how bleak the prospects, it is our duty as men and women who would make heroes of ourselves to become a banner of that unconquerable spirit that resists hardship, and is unbreakable in the face of extreme adversity. Archetypes of Invictus, we ride eternal into the teeth of the storm, into the heart of the battle, to seek out our enemy and break him with the hammer of courageous action. Awaken! Shake off your weakened state and rekindle the flame that once blazed in your breast — roar at this filthy world: "I will not be beaten by anything that you are capable of placing in my way.

Scarred and bloody, I will trod you under my steadfast footstep as I make my way ever further toward my glorious destiny!"

Through laughter and through tears, our actions must remain true. We must always Keep the Faith — in ourselves, in our Will, in our destiny. Our lives should grow into myths, and we should believe in ourselves with a religious fervor that would put a suicide bomber to shame, always convinced that our path is a righteous one, and our goals worthy. We should ensure the Truth is upheld in lives by our every word and deed, for there are those who rely on us, who come after us, following in our footsteps — it is our duty to them to not falter!

I say to you, whether you set out to lift weights or to create a new religion, your resolve must be the same. Every action is Holy. Every word is a gospel upon which all your future glories hang. If there are those who hold you back from your destiny, sever ties with them. If there are those who stand in your way, break them. If there are those who slander or mock you in the marketplace, ignore them, or crush them utterly. There is no between. There is no middle ground to hold in this war of life — the endless struggle calls for fanaticism, not luke-warm believers or fair-weather warriors.

Our bywords are Iron and Blood — that which makes us strong, and that which makes us who we are. That which is a weapon, and that which wields it. Arise! Awaken! Know that you are a furious and savage beast capable of the mightiest feats of awful glory, and that it is in your hands to control your fate — you hold the rudder, and no one else. You write this saga with every day you remain alive — let it be one of sex and blood and death and vengeance and love and hatred and utter victory. Hail to the ones who hold true! 92.

# XXXVIII.
# YOUR EXCUSES
# ARE WEAK AS FUCK

## TRANSMISSION DATE: 08-27-15

Everyone has heard them, everyone has made them:

*"I've tried, but I just can't seem to lose weight."*

*"I used to train but I hurt my knee/shoulder/back/vagina."*

*"I'm super busy. I just don't have the time."*

*"I have trouble staying motivated."*

*"It's too hard."*

*"I don't know where to begin."*

*"What's the point?"*

Excuses generally exhibit one of three different negative modes of thinking — hopelessness, helplessness and worthlessness. Training guru John Schaeffer identifies these behaviors as "the first meaning "it can't be done," the second meaning "it can be done, but I can't do it," and the third meaning, "it can be done and I can do it, but why should I be the one to do it?" Each of them is a victim mentality — suggesting that something outside of oneself is limiting one's ability to achieve a goal, and that the individual cannot control those outside elements to create a favorable environment in which change can occur. This is not limited to fitness training in any way- it exists across every facet of life, and will rear its ugly head constantly if one allows these poisoned thoughts to take root in their mind. At all times, and in all places, we must remember: WE ARE IN CONTROL OF OUR OWN LIVES. We must not allow ourselves to be seduced by victimhood! It is so attractive to many to have an "easy out" in every difficult area of life, some prepared excuse that will answer any challenge to why they are living in such an inglorious fashion.

I have heard of more maladies and specific ailments in the last few years than I can wrap my mind around (usually from the female end of the spectrum — sorry, ladies), that one would think that 7 out every 10 women are afflicted with a thyroid condition, fibromyalgia, or some kind of rare disease that doesn't allow their body to make positive change — regardless of whether they would stop drinking their beloved soft drinks or eating like a starving tribesman at McDonald's for the first time. An intense conditioning routine is simply out of the question. The actual likelihood of a legitimate thyroid condition is less than 5 percent. There are only an estimated 5 million people in the United States with fibromyalgia — of this number, 90% of those who complain of "muscle pain and fatigue" (the symptoms of fibromyalgia) and are diagnosed with fibro are women. I am not saying that there are not legitimate sufferers of chronic pain and fatigue, nor am I saying that thyroid conditions do not exist. I am saying that not all who claim to be affected by them, in fact, are. Many are subscribing to another easy method of victimization so prevalent in our culture today, and opting out of a life of trial and ordeal by simply saying "I can't." Men, you are not exempt. I have heard the "injury" excuse a thousand times, be that a bad shoulder, blown knees, a bad back, what have you. In many of these cases, the sufferer has not even attempted intelligent rehabilitation of the area in question, but has simply ceased training, and now uses his injury as a fall-back for why he has a beer gut and no motivation to not be a physical specimen of what it might look like if a manatee was crossed with your average football enthusiast. Rehabilitate your injury. Work around your injury. If your shoulder is hurt, work toward fixing that problem, while in the meantime, pursuing training that focuses more heavily on the lower body, or reducing body fat. Barring a serious condition, there is always something that can be done to make forward progress. The most common of all, however, and the most bullshit-filled, is the simple "I do not have time." The people that I hear say this are often telling me this in bar, on a facebook post, in between watching the game. If someone will look me dead in the eye and tell me that they are so efficient at managing their time that they literally do not have 10 spare minutes in the day to perform circuit training or sprints, and mean it, then I applaud them for being the most completely self-deluded person on the planet. There should be an award, maybe in the form of a pre-tied noose. With as little as 10 minutes a day, one can make forward progress in strength, conditioning and body composition. With even less than that, the question is, "what do you think is better, exercising for 5 minutes a day, or exercising for zero minutes a day?" "I don't have time." Fuck off and save your fucking excuses for a sympathetic ear, like one of your dozen cats, during your marathon sessions of Netflix and Cheeto consumption. "I don't know where to begin." Perhaps one of the only partially legitimate excuses out there, but so easily remedied that it is instantly rendered as useless as the rest. Go train with a friend, read a few articles, watch a damn youtube video and get going. Anything is better than nothing. If you are serious about getting started on the road to becoming a physical temple of glory, a shrine of strength and beauty, and would like some motivation, information and coaching, get in touch at grimnir1984@gmail.com. I offer distance coaching and personal training, which will further remove both obstacle and excuse from your life, and get you headed in the right direction towards concrete results and revolutionizing your life through total reform.

*"It is not faith in eternal life which guides me now, but the fact that I know I've not long to live- none have long for this world. So seize every night, every waking hour. Breathe every moment."*

None of us gets forever. We only have right now. Don't waste it on weakness. Spend it wisely on the path to glory. 92!

# XXXIX.
# SPAWN OF THE IRON WOOD

TRANSMISSION DATE: 09-20-15

*"Servants of the First Wolf, walking among men*
*Our cult is Fire and Frenzy — our Lord is Death.*
*We are Fear, Might, Ecstasy and Rage;*
*Crowned Kings of Violence and Power,*
*Breathlessly charging toward the Final Hour."*

Werewolf Divisions worldwide; Solo Operatives; those elite few who have been chosen to move from the Werewolf Operation into full-fledged Wolfdom — bearing now on their back the proclamation "WOLVES", one day to proudly wear that dread Wolf-banner beneath it, blood spattered white on a field of black — all of you are Sons of Perdition!

Our mission is a multi-pronged attack on the precepts and ideals of this age, what some have called the Kali Yuga, the Iron Age, but that we call the Wolf Age. We call it thus, because it is only the Wolves who can end it, our sharp teeth gnashing against the weakness and depravity both in our own lives and in the world at large. We call it thus, because this age both reviles and produces Wolves — at the edges of this crumbling Empire, we are in the woods, howling songs of destruction against our hated foes, making our bodies and minds into weapons capable of surviving the war against weakness.

Here on the perimeter of the rotten carcass called "modernity," we are making ourselves into archons —absolute rulers of ourselves, our souls and bodies— high priests in the wooded temples of our religion. This religion is the Wolf-Cult, both ancient in its inception and newly born again, roaring, glorious, vital, dangerous.

We have always been Wolves. Our kind has always banded together — it is in our blood to herald the death of an age, and to build a new on the ruins of the old, before that which we have created, too, is overthrown if it becomes weak in years to come.

The Operative's symbol on the Werewolf banner, called by us "Totenwolf," or "death-wolf," is the three-fold symbol of the Spawn of Ironwood. Wolf, Death, Serpent — the three children of ruinous destiny, agents of the destruction of the world as it was, heralds of a new/old way in which men and women worship strength in the place of weakness, heroism in the place of victimhood, healthiness in the place of sickness — but in order to do so, Solve must be the forerunner of Coagula.

Destroy the self. Re-forge the Self. Look deep within and find there the hidden wisdom and Will through which we will conquer. Rend yourself into pieces and identify those which are strong, those which are unhealthy. Purify. Distill. Re-arrange and re-create, until where once stood a man, now stands a symbol. Our legions will carry the battle standard to glory, but the victory must first be an internal one.

Those dedicated few who look for more involvement can make contact and join our ranks, first as a soldier in the Werewolf Operation, and from there, they must set their sights on creating Divisions, making the physical journeys to forge bonds with others, and swearing pacts with those Wolves met along the way. The time is now for the tribes to join under one banner — and this consanguineous union, we call Operation Werewolf. 92!

WWW.OPERATIONWEREWOLF.COM

Printed in Great Britain
by Amazon